A Manual of Construction Documentation

An Illustrated Guide to Preparing Construction Drawings

Glenn E. Wiggins AIA

WHITNEY LIBRARY OF DESIGN
An imprint of Watson-Guptill Publications/New York

First published in New York by Whitney Library of Design
an imprint of Watson-Guptill Publications,
Nielsen Business Media, a division of The Nielsen Company
770 Broadway, New York, NY 10003
www.watsonguptill.com

Library of Congress Cataloging-in-Publication Data
Wiggins, Glenn E.
   A manual of construction documentation / Glenn E. Wiggins.
      p.   cm.
   Includes index.
   ISBN 0–8230–3001–6. — ISBN 0–8230–3002–4 (pbk.)
   1. Architecture—Designs and plans—Working drawings.
2. Architecture—Designs and plans—Documentation.   I. Title.
NA2713.W54   1989
720′.28′4—dc19   88-38846
                                          CIP

Manufactured in U.S.A.

First printing, 1989

11 12 13 14 15 / 10 09 08

*My thanks to Rae Jean Nicholas Wiggins
for her counsel during the preparation of this book.*

Contents

Introduction

Construction documentation is the process of communicating architectural designs to builders, fabricators, and all others who will execute the architect's designs. The products of this process are the working drawings and schedules—created according to recognized conventions—that comprise a standard set of construction documents.

In most architectural offices, between 40 and 50 percent of a project fee typically will be allocated to preparing construction documents. Thus, for any given project, almost half of an architect's time will be spent on construction documentation. Poor skills in this area will hurt almost any practicing architect. Even that small percentage of practitioners who will be involved only with design will benefit from a knowledge of construction documentation, as it will help them to communicate more clearly with those who are preparing the construction documents.

This book presents a consistent method of creating a set of construction documents. It utilizes as an example a medium-size, two-story speculative office building. This building is not meant to be "high-design." Rather, it has been made intentionally simple in order to make the information clear and to reinforce the highly graphic presentation of information.

Once you learn the system described in this book, you can use it on virtually any type or size of commercial building—with some modifications, depending on the requirements of the project.

Each chapter represents a unique type of information that becomes part of a set of construction documents. On some projects this may mean that one or more sheets will need to be drafted for each type of information; on other projects, this may mean that one sheet can be used to show two or more types of information. For example, on smaller jobs it is not uncommon to combine window frame types with door and/or finish schedules.

Within each chapter, this information is broken into three sections. The first contains the necessary background information for a particular class of drawing; the next provides the set of graphic symbols that are appropriate for the drawing or drawings represented;

and the final section presents a series of drawings which represent drafting phases. This series graphically illustrates the sequence in which information is placed onto a particular drawing. On each drawing the black items represent new information, while the blue items represent information previously drawn.

It is important for a set of construction documents to be developed in a certain sequence. For example, there is no need to have a completed sheet of window frame types before the exterior elevation sheet has been started. It is also important to observe sequencing so that project consultants will be assured of receiving the information that they will require in order to provide you with timely feedback and to complete their part of the documentation. With experience, the rationale behind this sequencing will become increasingly clear.

This book is appropriate and important for at least two groups of people. The first group is composed of students and interns who are hoping to enter, or who have already entered, the architectural profession. Because it is intended to be a guide for people in the early stages of learning, certain elements that are difficult to anticipate or that occur infrequently—such as those often occurring in large-scale projects—are not included.

The second group of users consists of architectural offices that are in need of a set of reference standards. Offices generally prefer for the style and approach of their drawings to be consistent. Toward this end, many offices develop standards for their staffs to follow. However, these standards are often incomplete. This book provides a complete set of standards that can be used by all office employees.

It is important to remember that in construction documentation there is not one right way. What is important is consistency and clarity within a given system. This book presents one consistent and clear system which, once learned, can always be amended to meet any variations that a particular office or individual might prefer.

One final note: This book works in tandem with the author's *Construction Details for Commercial Buildings* (Whitney Library of Design, 1988) to the extent that some of the details from that book are used as the examples here.

1 General Utility Information

This chapter provides background information necessary for preparing a good set of construction documents. While this book is not about drawing techniques, there are some tips that you will find helpful in documentation, the best of which may be to study the methods shown in this book's sample documents. If, for example, there is a question about line weight for a specific element of a drawing, refer to the sample document as a model. By following this process, you will begin to develop a consistent system of documentation. Again, consistency and clarity are critical.

■ Drawings to Include in a Set of Documents

The best way to begin looking at a set of construction documents is to break it down into its major components. You will then see that there are actually only eleven components to be documented. These components, which make up the individual chapters of this book, are:

1. Site plans
2. Floor plans
3. Roof plans
4. Reflected ceiling plans
5. Exterior elevations
6. Building sections
7. Wall sections
8. Vertical transportation
9. Enlarged plans and interior elevations
10. Schedules
11. Details

Also included in an overall set of construction documents is the project specification, an 8½-by-11-inch bound document of written instructions and requirements. This specification is broken down by division according to standards set forth by the Construction Specifications Institute (CSI). Its purpose is to convey methods, materials, standards, responsibilities, and specific product-selection data. The production of specifications is not covered in this book.

On small- and medium-scale projects, each of the first ten components of a construction document set will usually require only a single sheet in order to properly convey the required information. The eleventh component, detailing, is generally assembled into a bound 8½-by-11-inch document, which shall be referred to as the detail book. Some offices, however, prefer to put details directly onto larger sheets.

■ Graphic and Informational Elements

In drafting, there are certain elements that should always be consistent. By using the following set of standards, different team members are able to work on the same set of drawings.

Lettering

One of the most personal skills that architects work to acquire is lettering. However, overly personalized lettering presents two problems. First, it is important that lettering on construction documents be neat and easy to read. This means that lettering styles with too much flair will need to be toned down for construction documentation. Second, it is better for team projects if the lettering of every member of the team has more or less the same style. This gives the documents greater consistency.

Toward this goal of consistency, it is a good practice to use a lettering guide that can be slipped under a drawing and used for its guidelines. This lettering guide will help you to achieve a consistent size of lettering, a neater drawing, and an increase in production speed. A blank lettering guide is included in Appendix A. Lettering should fit neatly into the guidelines, and all verticals should be drawn with a small triangle. The following examples show two different styles of lettering, either of which is acceptable. It should be stressed, however, that once you select a style of lettering, you should maintain it throughout the entire set of construction documents.

The all-upper-case style of lettering shown here is used commonly in many architectural offices.

A BCDEFGHIJKLMNOPQRSTUVWXYZ

The all-lower-case style of lettering below is less common than the upper-case style, but is the personal preference of many.

abcdefghijklmnopqrstuvwxyz

Most people who letter poorly do so because of lack of practice. By practicing for thirty minutes, four days a week, you will improve your lettering dramatically. The best way to practice is to trace another person's lettering. Eventually, your own style will emerge.

Grouping of Notes and Style of Note Leaders

On any drawing it is important to group and align notes in a logical fashion. Note leaders, which lead the eye from the note to the item that is being referenced, should never cross, and should lead away from either the beginning or end of the note. These leaders should be drawn with a French curve; they should not be straight lines, as straight leaders can be easily confused with elements of the drawing. With practice these rules will become second nature.

The figure below illustrates the features of good noting. The broken lines show how the notes have been aligned. The leader lines have been drawn with a French curve and start at either the beginning or end of each note.

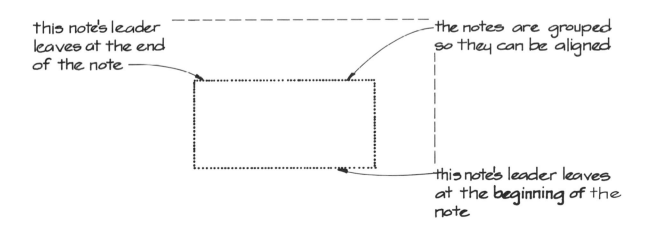

this note's leader leaves at the end of the note

the notes are grouped so they can be aligned

this note's leader leaves at the beginning of the note

Sheet Numbers, Drawing Numbers, and Drawing Titles

There are many ways to number sheets of drawings. For example, on larger-scale projects you might number all of the drawings dealing with particular elements of the set by a 100 series number. All drawings dealing with site plans would receive a 100 series number, all drawings dealing with floor plans would receive a 200 series number, and so forth. On small- and medium-scale projects, however, numbering sequentially by discipline is appropriate. Architectural drawing numbers are preceded by an "A" (e.g., A-1, A-2, A-3), structural drawing numbers are preceded by an "S" (e.g., S-1, S-2, S-3), and so forth with mechanical drawings preceded by an "M" and electrical drawings preceded by an "E".

Every drawing that occurs on a sheet should receive a number, title, and scale. For any type of "plan" drawing (site plans, floor plans, and so forth), a north arrow will also be required. Drawings such as elevations, sections, and details do not require a north arrow. When there are multiple drawings on a sheet, the numbering should be started with "1" in the upper right-hand corner and move to the left in horizontal rows. Drawings that require a north arrow should have it drawn to the immediate right of the number, followed by the title and scale. Again, the sizes shown are not rigid standards. It is more important to be consistent once a size has been selected.

For drawings that do not require a north arrow, the title and scale should be drawn to the immediate right of the number.

Using a template when drafting titles helps to increase consistency in the documents. Please note that the sizes of template lettering shown in this book are not rigid standards—any template system that makes use of these general sizes is acceptable. Hand lettering is also acceptable. Press-on-lettering should be avoided on working drawings, as it is subject to too much abuse to be sufficiently durable.

Sheet Composition

As previously mentioned, it is good practice to position information drafted on a sheet on the right-hand side. There are several reasons for this. When a set of drawings is assembled, it is typically bound on the left-hand side, which means that at least 1½ inches of the left-hand side of each sheet will be lost. Therefore, even on crowded sheets, nothing should be drawn any closer to the left-hand side than 2½ inches.

The fact that sets are bound on the left-hand side also means that information on the right-hand side of the sheets will be seen first by a person turning the sheets in a set of construction documents. For example, when you are using floor plans, you may need to reference a wall section. Turning back and forth from one page to another, you will work more quickly if the important information occurs on the right-hand side of the sheet. By the same reasoning, on sheets with multiple drawings, it is good practice to locate those elements that are the most typical and that will be referenced the most on the right-hand side of the sheet. Less typical elements can be drafted toward the left-hand side.

On sheets that will have numerous drawings, it is best to start drawing in the upper-right-hand corner and proceed to the left-hand side of the sheet. On sheets with only one item of information on the sheet, the drawing should still be placed toward the right-hand side of the sheet. If possible, you should also locate the drawing(s) slightly above the center of the sheet to leave room at the bottom for general notes and other miscellaneous information.

Abbreviations

Typically abbreviations should be avoided. However, when certain words are repeated frequently on a drawing, or when there is a limited amount of space available for notes, abbreviations may be used. It is important, however, to use abbreviations that are generally recognized in the profession. You should not create abbreviations of your own. A set of accepted abbreviations is included in Appendix A.

Material Indications

Material indications, or poché, are added to drawings to make them more graphically precise. The amount of material indication that any drawing receives will often depend on the amount of time the drafter has. If time is short, certain drawings may be complete without material indications. As a rule, however, it is preferable to draw material indications on all construction documents.

Material indications should be taken from standards that are generally recognized in the profession; avoid creating your own symbols. Although some architects will develop pages of symbols to be used for material indications, simple symbols are the most effective. A set of recognized material indications is included in Appendix A.

Front versus Back of the Sheet

When drafting on mylar or good-quality vellum, you have the option of drawing on the front or the back of the sheet. At first the concept of drawing on the back of the sheet may seem a little odd, but in some cases it can be advantageous.

Column centerlines should be drawn on the back side of the sheet. By the time construction documents are started for a given project, you can usually be certain that the structural bay sizes will not change. By drafting the centerlines for these bays onto the back of the sheet they will be become "permanent," and will not be erased if other items are erased. For example, it would be realistic to assume that a 3⅝-inch metal stud interior partition would form one wall of a corridor running the entire length of a building and that the partition would be located exactly on a column centerline. If midway through the project you need to move this partition by 7 inches, you will need to erase and redraft both the partition and the centerline. If you draft the centerline on the back of the sheet, however, you will only need to redraft the partition. Although this may seem like a trivial point, it can save a great deal of time and irritation through the course of construction documentation. The column centerlines form the basic reference for the entire set of construction documents. Each time they are erased and redrafted represents not only a waste of time, but also a point where critical mistakes can be made.

Material indications should also be drafted on the back of the sheet. There are two reasons for this. The first deals with revisions. It is not unusual to change materials for components of an assembly very late in a project's documentation. For example, assume that all of the wall sections and parapet details for a project have been drawn and noted as using ¾-inch plywood for the exterior exposure of the parapet. Then, at the last minute, the contractor suggests that a significant cost savings can be realized if the plywood is changed to gypsum sheathing. Assuming that the architect has no reasonable objection to this revision, the material indication will need to be changed on the documents. If the material indication has been drafted on the back side of the sheet, this change is very quick and easy. If, however, the material indications have been drawn on the front side of the sheet, the change may be tedious, as you would have to erase very small areas of plywood material indication while not disturbing any of the adjacent drawing.

The second reason for drafting material indications on the back of the sheet is more subtle. When mylar sheets are printed as bluelines, the mylar is placed right side up onto the print side of the blueline paper. This means that items on the back of the sheet will actually be printed slightly darker and sharper than items on the front of the sheet. This small difference allows you to draw material indications very lightly on the back of a sheet with the assurance that they will be sharp when printed, without overpowering the remainder of the drawing.

■ The Mock-Up Set

Before you start a set of construction documents, there is already a tremendous amount of work that has been done and information that has been accumulated. A code analysis should be available for reference to confirm that the building meets the required codes. Preliminary information should be available from the engineering consultants concerning their parts of the project's documentation. Design development drawings will be available that will show all of the architectural design features of the building.

The first step toward preparing construction documents, therefore, is to take all of the known information and create a mock-up set of documents. The purpose of this mock-up set is to determine, before any drafting is done, where all items to be included in the set will be located within the set of documents. Mock-up sets are generally drawn at one quarter or one half of the full size.

Each drawing that will be a part of the final construction documents set is drawn onto a mock-up sheet more or less to scale, but as an empty box that is labeled with a drawing number, title, and scale. This allows you to plan the sheet composition and to reduce the risk of overlooking important drawings.

For example, assume that in doing the mock-up sheet for exterior elevations you decide that you will need to draw three of the building façades to properly convey your design and construction intent. One rectangle should be drawn onto the mock-up sheet for each elevation. The rectangle should generally be the size of the elevation being drawn, and should be located where you want the final elevation to be drawn. Underneath each of these rectangles you should insert the drawing number, title, and scale.

Thus, at the beginning of the construction documentation you will already have your exterior elevation sheet planned. Other sheets are done similarly until the entire set has been "mocked up," and all eleven components of information have been documented.

On smaller jobs, assembling a mock-up set may seem like a poor use of time. It is, however, a good practice to establish. On larger scale projects it is possible that exterior elevations might require a dozen or more sheets. In these cases, the mock-up is a tremendous organizational asset.

■ Typical Sheet Title Block

Title blocks for sheets can be very complicated or quite simple. Composition of the title block is largely a personal matter. An example is shown at the right. Items that should be considered as minimums for inclusion would be:

1. Project name
2. Project location
3. Client name
4. Architect name
5. Consultant names
6. Issue block
7. Space for architect's seal
8. Date
9. Sheet title
10. Sheet number

A
SPECULATIVE
OFFICE
BUILDING
in
DUGONE COUNTY
for

NICHOLAS
PROPERTIES

GENW, PC.
architect

BUILDINGS R US
engineers

ISSUE:

DATE:

2 Site Plans

Site plans are generally started very early in the process of preparing a set of construction documents. This helps the consultants on the job by providing them with information that is necessary for their work to progress. It also helps the architect by getting some of the drafting work done before the final phase of the project. Site plans generally do not contain a great deal of cross-references to other drawings in the document set, but they do contain references to a number of details that will need to be prepared for the detail book.

■ General Information

Site plans can be among the simplest or the most complex construction drawings to execute. The degree of difficulty will depend on the extent of work that the architect chooses to do personally. There are three distinct parts to a site plan; the architectural site plan, the landscape site plan, and the grading site plan. One or all of these site plans may be done by the architect. If two or more parts are done by the architect, it may be necessary to break the information out onto separate sheets. This decision will be based on an evaluation of the amount of information that a sheet can hold while still providing clarity, the expected bidding procedures, and personal preference.

The architectural site plan shows features of the site that are of architectural importance, as opposed to features that would be important for landscaping or grading purposes. Also included would be engineering features that would have an architectural impact, such as transformers, exterior lighting, fire hydrants, and so forth.

The landscape site plan shows features that are of importance to the landscaping contractor. A detailed listing of all plant materials should be included that shows plant type, size, and quantity desired. Notes covering the fates of existing trees and shrubs should also be included on the plan. On some simpler projects this plan may be combined with the architectural site plan. Frequently, however, this drawing will be prepared by an outside consultant and will not be included as a construction document that is prepared by the architect. Therefore, information about landscape site plans is not included in this book.

The grading site plan shows the grading aspects of the site. On certain simpler projects this plan may be combined with the architectural site plan. Frequently, however, as is the case with the landscape site plan, the grading site plan will be prepared by an outside consultant and will not be included as a construction document supplied by the architect. In addition to information about the grading of the site, the grading site plan also must include two general notes. The first note provides the date that the survey for the site was performed and the name of the group that did the work. The second note makes reference to the soils report for the project, stating that said report, although not bound into the set of construction documents, should be considered a part of the set.

When drafting a site plan, you should imagine taking an aerial photograph of the site. The exception to this view is the building itself. Although some architects like to draft the roof of the building onto the site plan and thus remove the need to draft a separate roof plan, it is preferable to separate the two drawings for a clearer presentation. When using this method, you should draft a heavy outline of the building's footprint onto the site plan.

Site plans should be shown at a scale that will provide an adequate and clear presentation of all of the required information. You should note that site plans make use of engineers' scales instead of architects' scales. Appropriate scales include, but are not limited to, $1" = 20'-0"$ and $1" = 40'-0"$.

In dimensioning site plans it is typical to use decimal notation rather than feet and inches. Although not a rigid requirement, decimal notation is the general convention within the building profession. Using decimal notation will also make it easier for you to cross-reference the numerous types of site plans. Dimensions indicated should be the actual dimensions. (For more information on dimensioning systems see Chapter 3, "Floor Plans.")

Site plans should always be oriented on a sheet in such a way that the north arrow is pointing either up or to the right (pointing up is the most typical orientation). This is the convention in the building and engineering professions. The site plan should be located slightly above and to the right of the center of the sheet. This allows space at the bottom of the sheet for notes to be added if necessary. Also, as has been noted in Chapter 1, it is a good practice to direct information away from the left-hand (binding) edge of the sheet.

■ Appropriate Notes and Symbols
These notes and symbols are broken into two categories: architectural site plan and grading site plan.

Architectural Site Plan •
The property line for the site should be shown as a series of long heavy lines with two dashes. The information concerning the location of the property line should be taken from the site survey.

A heavy outline of the building's footprint should be shown.

The finished floor elevation of the ground level should be clearly labeled inside of this footprint with a bullet.

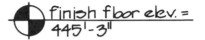

finish floor elev. = 445'-3"

All names of streets that adjoin the property should be labeled with a lettering style that is slightly larger and bolder than the standard.

(standard) main st.

All utility lines as well as power poles, transformers, traffic signals, and manholes should be copied from the survey onto the site plan.

All concrete walks should have their expansion joints drafted and labeled "EJ." Contraction joints should also be drafted but need not be labeled. (Expansion joints are typically around ½" thick and will run all of the way through the concrete walk. Contraction, or relief, joints are tooled joints that are around ⅛" wide and ¾" deep. Expansion joints should be spaced at a maximum of 25'-0" while contraction joints should be spaced at a maximum of 6'-0". Unless precise spacing and location of joints is desired as a design feature, their spacing can be taken care of with a general note or a sentence in the project specification.)

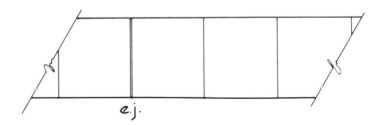

e.j.

Dimensions should be in generally continuous strings (ones that run for more or less the entire length of the drawing). Short strings should be avoided. Dimension strings that are intended to locate the building should intersect the property lines to give them a logical frame of reference. Dimension strings for other site features should intersect either the building or the property lines. When dimension lines intersect with items that are being referenced, they should be marked with a slash drawn at the 45-degree angle—for vertical dimensions from left to right and from right to left for horizontal dimensions.

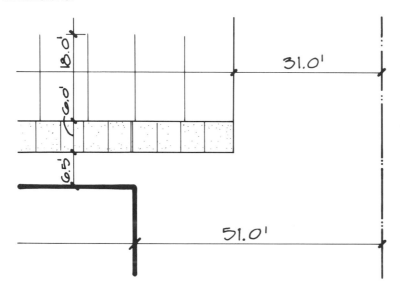

All exterior lighting, including lighting poles, bollards, and any specialty lighting should be drawn and referenced to the appropriate consultant's drawings.

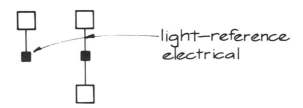

Other features that would be drawn on the architectural site plan include drives, gutters, curbs, signs, and so forth. All details should be referenced to the detail book by an arrow and a reference number. Some details, however, may be more appropriately referenced with a circle. The "DB" shown in the following drawings indicates that the marked detail has been included in the detail book. The first number refers to the section or chapter of the detail book that contains the detail, the second to the detail number within the specified chapter that shows the referenced detail.

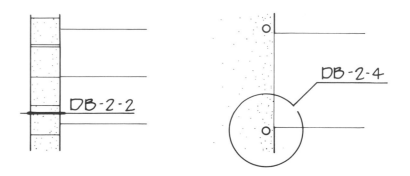

Radius information for curved parts of the site, such as parking islands or drives, should be indicated by an arrow that shows the radius as well as by a note "R=X," providing the length of the radius.

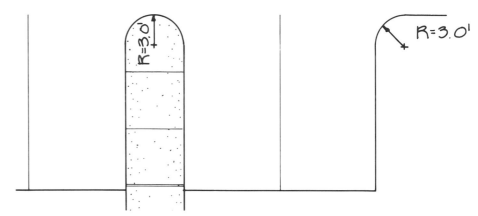

Grading Site Plan
Benchmark location and elevation should be clearly indicated with a bullet, the letters "BM," and the elevation in feet.

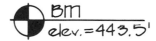

All existing grades should be shown. Existing grades should be drafted freehand as a series of light dashes.

All new grades should be shown. New grades are drafted freehand as a light line that is interrupted on occasion to indicate the elevation that it represents. Contour intervals will depend on the specific project site. A steep site would require more contours than would a level site.

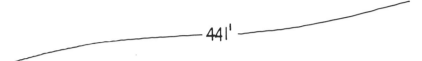

All existing spot elevations should be shown. These elevations are typically indicated by a cross, with the intersection of the cross representing the point that is being referenced.

All new spot elevations should be shown. These elevations are typically indicated by an angular leader terminating with a heavy dot. The dot represents the point being referenced.

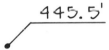

■ Sequence of the Documentation Procedure

The site plan is drafted in three phases. It is completed before most of the other drawings in the documents set, and thus does not have a fourth phase.

■ Phase I

As is the case with all construction documents, the first phase of the drawing usually requires the most actual drafting. The plus side of this is the fact that most of this initial work is relatively easy, as it is primarily an execution of known items from the design phase of the project.

The Phase I drawing shows the site and its property lines as well as the surrounding roadways. The general configuration of the parking is also shown. At this point the only architectural site feature shown is the preliminary outline of the concrete walk.

The drawing is next given its title and scale, and information in the title block is filled in properly. With this information complete, the site plan is now at a stage of completion that will allow the engineering consultants to begin more serious work on their parts of the construction document set.

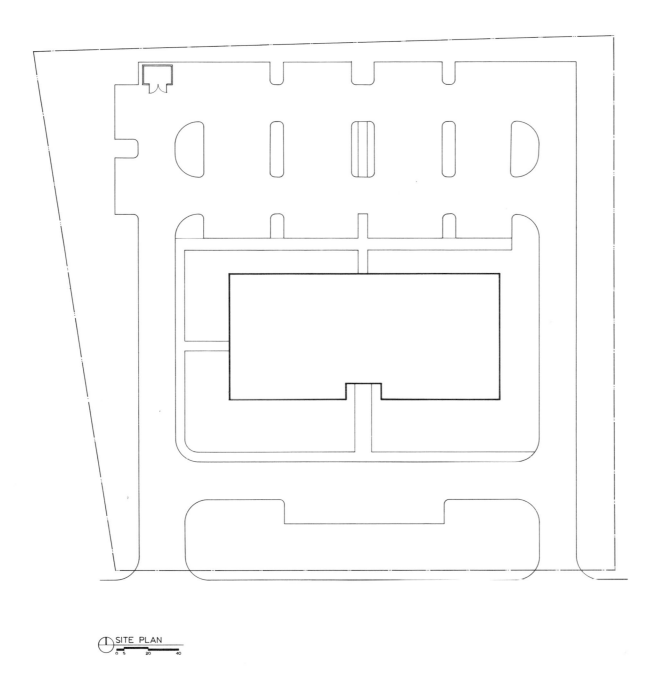

SITE PLAN

0 5   20   40

A
SPECULATIVE
OFFICE
BUILDING
in
DUGONE COUNTY
for

NICHOLAS
PROPERTIES

GEN W, PC.
architect

BUILDINGS R US
engineers

ISSUE:

DATE :

SITE PLAN

A - 1

21

■ Phase II

The second phase of the site plan documentation reflects a substantial step forward in terms of drawing refinement. The parking areas are completed and dimensioned (including radius information), the concrete walks are dimensioned and noted, and some of the architectural features such as benches are added.

Engineering features that will have a direct impact on the architectural nature of the project are added to the drawing at this stage. These include the locations of the transformer as well as site lighting.

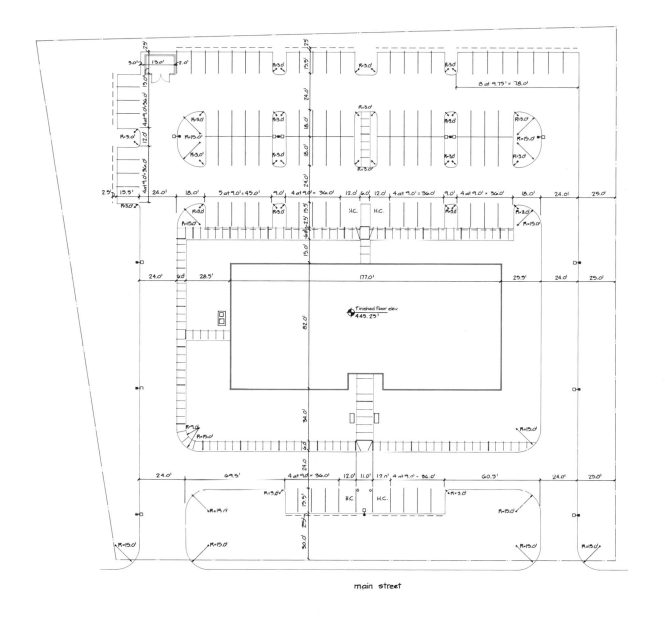

main street

SITE PLAN
0 5   20   40

A
SPECULATIVE
OFFICE
BUILDING
in
DUGONE COUNTY
for

NICHOLAS
PROPERTIES

GEN W, PC
architect

BUILDINGS R US
engineers

ISSUE:

DATE:

SITE PLAN

A-1

23

■ Phase III

This final phase of the site plan documentation reflects the addition of notes, detail cuts, and material indications. As you can see, the amount of work needed to do material indications for a site plan is rather modest. Still, if time were to become a constraint, material indications could be eliminated.

Detail cuts refer to details that would be drafted concurrent to the completion of the site plan for inclusion in the detail book. For the purposes of this book, the assumption is that the grading for the site has been performed by an outside consultant. Therefore, references to items such as manholes and catch basins are not included. If, however, the grading were to be incorporated onto the architectural site plan, these items would need to be included.

Miscellaneous notes are also added during this phase of the drawing. Included are the references to the soils report and to the survey. In the noting it is also important to include descriptions of any items that might not have been detailed previously due to time constraints. The reason for this is simple. When a set of construction documents is released for bid, the contractor estimates how much the project will cost to build based on the construction documents and the project specification. Typically, a contractor will be hired based on the bid that is given. Understandably, contractors are reluctant to "give away" items that were not originally included in the construction documents. Neither are owners generally anxious to spend more than the amount that was originally set forth in the contractor's bid. By including notes about undetailed items, the architect is assured that an allowance will be made for each item, and that items will not have to be eliminated because of an oversight.

You should check all documents at their final phase of completion, verifying all dimension strings and detail references.

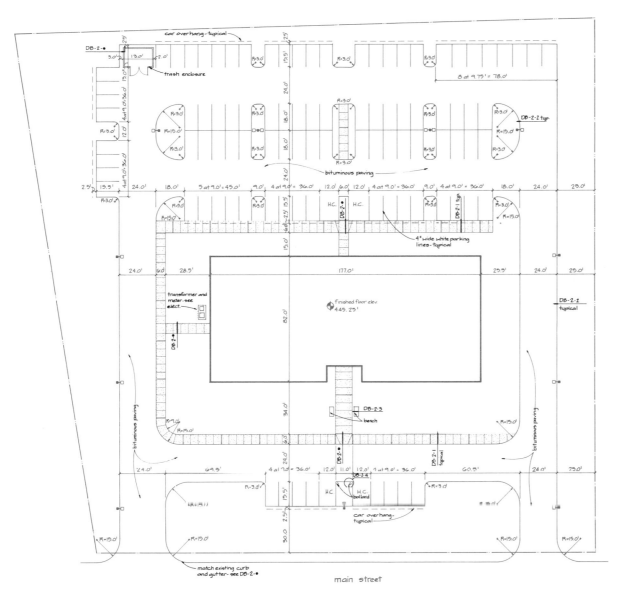

SITE PLAN
0 5   20   40

main street

A
SPECULATIVE
OFFICE
BUILDING
in
DUGONE COUNTY
for

NICHOLAS
PROPERTIES

GENW, PC.
architect

BUILDINGS R US
engineers

GENERAL NOTES AND SYMBOLS
all dimensions are actual to finished face

for landscaping features see landscape plan

for site grading, utilities, and elevation see civil

H.C. - handicap parking - stencil handicap symbol
onto bituminous paving with white paint

site lighting - see electrical

expansion joint - see DB-2-•

ISSUE

DATE:

SITE PLAN

A-1

25

■ **The Completed Site Plan**

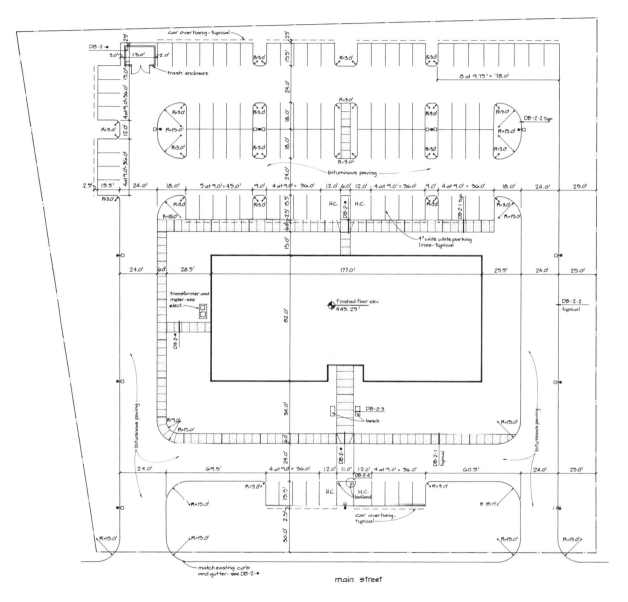

A
SPECULATIVE
OFFICE
BUILDING
in
DUGONE COUNTY
for

NICHOLAS
PROPERTIES

GENW, PC.
architect

BUILDINGS R US
engineers

GENERAL NOTES AND SYMBOLS
all dimensions are actual to finished face.

for landscaping features see landscape plan

for site grading, utilities, and elevation see civil

H.C. -handicap parking- stencil handicap symbol
onto bituminous paving with white paint

▪-□   site lighting- see electrical

⊔   expansion joint - see DB-2-●

ISSUE:

DATE:

SITE PLAN

A-1

SITE PLAN
0 5   20   40

main street

3 Floor Plans

Floor plans are the central, or core, drawings of any set of construction documents. They not only contain a tremendous amount of vital information for consultants and construction tradespeople, they also contain many cross-references to other parts of the documents. In a sense the floor plan is the directory for a set of documents. If the plan itself does not show the information you need, it typically will provide the appropriate reference to locate the desired information.

■ General Information

Because they play a critical role in the set of construction documents, floor plans are generally among the first, if not the first, drawings to be started. When drafting a floor plan, you should imagine looking down at the floor after the building has been sliced several feet above the finished floor being referenced. You see the tops of casework, plumbing fixtures, and other interior features as well as sections through exterior walls, interior partitions, and the structure.

Floor plans should be drawn at a scale that provides an adequate and clear presentation of all of the required information. The most common scales are $\frac{1}{16}'' = 1'\text{-}0''$, $\frac{1}{8}'' = 1'\text{-}0''$, and $\frac{1}{4}'' = 1'\text{-}0''$. Typically $\frac{1}{8}'' = 1'\text{-}0''$ will be the appropriate scale for a floor plan. The scale of $\frac{1}{4}'' = 1'\text{-}0''$ is used most commonly on enlarged plans (see Chapter 10, "Enlarged Plans and Interior Elevations"). However, in some cases, when the plan is rather small, the larger scale will be appropriate for the overall plan, thus removing the need for enlarged plans.

As with site plans, floor plans should always be oriented on a sheet in such a way that the north arrow is either pointing up or to the right, and should be located slightly above and to the right of the center of the sheet.

When drafting floor plans you should also include the major features of the site that are immediately adjacent to the building. This will help to tie the floor plan and the site plan together. Also, when drafting an upper-level floor plan that has an adjoining roof below, you should draw in accordance with the standards that are described in Chapter 4, "Roof Plans."

Before you select the appropriate items to be included on the floor plans, it is important to review methods of dimensioning architectural plans. There are three common methods of dimensioning that are used in commercial construction; framing (finish), actual, and nominal. Each method has its own strengths and weaknesses.

Framing dimensions relate to the actual size of the framing member that a dimension string is referencing. For example, a $3\frac{5}{8}''$ metal stud partition with $\frac{5}{8}''$ gypsum board applied to each side would be dimensioned on the floor plans as 3⅝". Similarly, a 7⅝" concrete block with ⅞" metal furring and ⅝" gypsum board applied to each side would be dimensioned as 7⅝". The strength of this system is that it tells the construction people in the field the dimension that is most immediately important to them. Because of construction sequencing, metal studs and masonry walls will be put in place well ahead of any interior finishes. The initial tradespeople that work on the project will not be concerned with final finishes.

Thus, by using framing dimensions, the architect has precise control over the locations of the walls.

The weakness of the framing-dimension system comes from the fact that control over framing locations does not necessarily extend to control over construction techniques. Although the architect will detail the precise construction required for interior partitions, the contractor may substitute certain materials or alter the desired method of construction. These changes may result in the partition wall having a slightly different thickness than was initially desired, which can cause improper clearances between walls or improper fit of interior finishes. These problems occur less when a good contractor is being used and the architect makes thorough field observations.

Actual, or finish, dimensioning corrects the potential problem described above. For example, a 3⅝" metal stud partition with ⅝" gypsum board applied to each side would be dimensioned on the floor plans as 4⅞". Similarly, a 7⅝" concrete block with ⅞" metal furring and ⅝" gypsum board applied to each side would be dimensioned as 10⅝". The strength of this system lies in the ability of the architect to control the finished dimensions of partitions and other architectural features. The detriment of the system lies in its failure to recognize the sequence of construction. Because framing will always be installed before finishes, the construction crew is required to do math when doing the framing work, dramatically increasing the probability of mistakes occurring in the process of locating the framing members. Although many architects would refer to this type of construction mistake as the "contractor's problem," it is wiser to restrict the use of actual dimensioning on floor plans to projects that are primarily interior architecture.

Nominal dimensioning is a mutation of framing dimensioning and is used primarily to eliminate fractions that are considered unimportant in the field. For example, a 3⅝" metal stud partition with ⅝" gypsum board applied to each side would be dimensioned on the floor plans as 4". Similarly, a 7⅝" concrete block with ⅞" metal furring and ⅝" gypsum board applied to each side would be dimensioned as 8". The strength of this system is the elimination of many fractions in the dimensions. In construction, it is not realistic to expect elements of a project to be built any closer than 1⁄16" to the dimension that is indicated on the drawing. Some variance in the constructed dimension is to be expected. (Even a tolerance of ⅛" is considered extreme by some professionals.)

Thus, on a project that has many interior features whose locations can vary slightly, the nominal system of dimensioning has many advantages. It does, however, combine both of the weaknesses of the two previously described systems. It requires math in the field (as fractions must be reinstated when actual dimensions are needed), thus increasing the likelihood of error, and it does not specifically locate the framing member.

The floor plans in this book use the framing dimension system. Different drawings, however, will frequently use different dimension systems. A ceiling plan, for example, will generally use actual dimensioning because of the sequencing of construction (see Chapter 5, "Reflected Ceiling Plans"). Remember, it is always important on any plan to include a general note that describes the system of dimensioning that is being used for the particular drawing.

■ Appropriate Notes and Symbols
Finished floor elevations should be clearly labeled with a bullet. All level changes that take place on a given floor should be indicated. Ramp elevation changes should be shown in feet and inches with spot elevations.

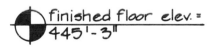

Dimensions should be in generally continuous strings. Short strings should be avoided. When a dimension string intersects a column centerline, the intersection should be marked with a dot. When a dimension string intersects any other feature, that intersection should be marked with a slash drawn at a 45-degree angle. This slash should slope from left to right for vertical dimensions and from right to left for horizontal dimensions.

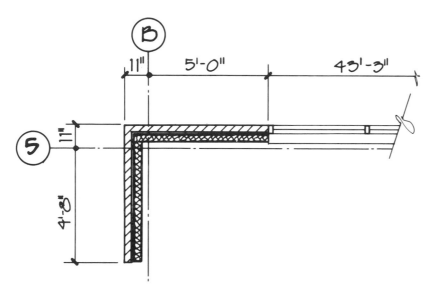

Column centerlines and column designation bubbles should be drafted in such a way that the centerline runs through the entire floor plan. Drafted as a series of long lines with single dashes, the column centerlines form the basic reference point for all dimension lines. The size of the centerline bubble should be appropriate for the designation to be labeled within it. All bubbles should be the same size; they should be located at the top of the floor plan for horizontal dimensions and to the right-hand side of the floor plan for vertical dimensions. Bubbles should be drafted several inches from the floor plan to allow space for dimension lines.

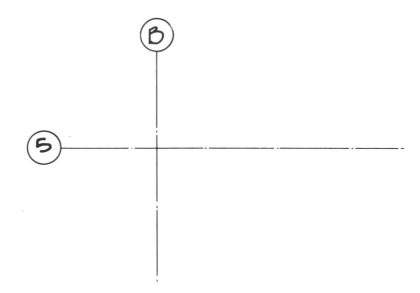

Partition type detail cuts are drawn as a short line with a slightly thickened section at the point of intersection with the wall. Above the short line is written a number, which refers to the partition type in the detail book. The letters "DB" indicate that the marked detail is included in the detail book. The first number refers to the section or chapter of the detail book that contains the detail, and the second number refers to the detail number within the specified chapter.

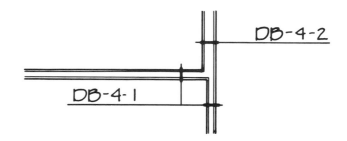

Cross-referencing cuts—wall sections. The arrow symbol shown refers to a wall section that is located on another sheet within the set of construction documents. Underneath the arrow is a number to help locate the section. The first number refers to the sheet number, while the second number refers to the particular drawing on the sheet. The size of the arrowhead is not critical, although once a size has been selected, it should be held consistent. A good system for drawing arrows is to make the bottom of the arrow a minimum of ⅜″ and to draw the sides with the 30-degree side of a 30/60 triangle.

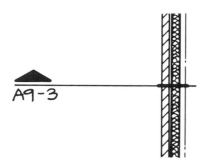

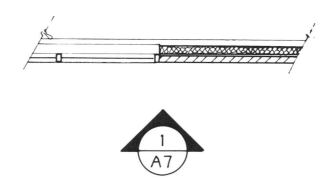

Cross-referencing cuts—building section. The symbol shown below is used to refer to a building section that is located on another sheet within the set of construction documents. The bottom number refers to the sheet number, while the top number refers to the particular drawing on the sheet. The size of the circle should be such that it can easily contain the information that is labeled inside of it. Once a size is selected, all circles should be held consistent and adhere to the standard.

Cross-referencing cuts—enlarged plans. Enlarged plans are large-scale drawings of parts of floor plans that appear separately in the document set. Typically, to save time and to avoid redundancy, you will not go into any detail describing a part of a plan that is being enlarged elsewhere. This is true not only for notes, but also for dimensions. Enlarged plans are referenced by showing a series of heavy broken lines around the part of the floor plan that is being enlarged. The numbering system is standard, with the top number referring to the specific drawing and the bottom number referring to the sheet where the drawing occurs.

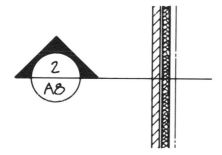

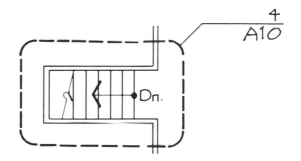

Cross-referencing cuts—elevation. This next symbol refers to an exterior or interior elevation that is located on another sheet within the set of construction documents. The bottom number refers to the sheet number, while the top number refers to the particular drawing on the sheet. The size of the circle should be such that it can easily contain the information that is labeled inside of it. Once a size is selected, all circles should be held constant and adhere to the standard.

Door types are indicated by a number in an ellipse shape in or near the door swing. The first number in the ellipse designates the room number in which the door occurs, and the letter following that number represents the specific door within the given room (see Chapter 11). The size of the ellipse should be adequate to provide for a clear labeling of all needed information. Once a size is selected, all ellipses should adhere to the standard.

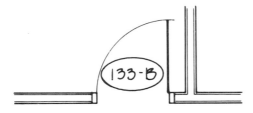

Room names and numbers should be drawn in slightly larger and bolder lettering than standard. Every room should receive a name and a number, with the basement starting the 000 series, the street level starting the 100 series, the second level starting the 200 series, and so forth. If a room number and name will not fit into the room itself, they should be located close to the room with a leader referencing them appropriately.

Where changes in floor finishes occur, they should be shown and noted. The division should be indicated with an "X" arrowhead and the immediate area at the division should be rendered appropriately (see page 13 for information on material indications). Changes in floor finishes need not be indicated graphically when the changes occur at door openings.

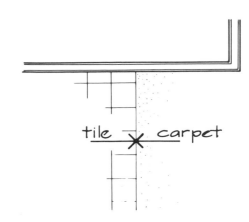

Other features that should be shown on the floor plan might include casework, floor drains, plumbing fixtures, floor mats, and structural columns. All architectural details should be referenced to the detail book by either a cut arrow with a reference number or a reference circle with a reference number.

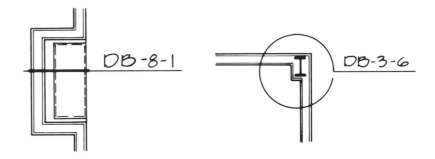

All materials should be properly indicated in accordance with the standards described in Chapter 1.

■ Sequence of the Documentation Procedure

The documents for both the first and the second level plans are included as examples of floor plan documentation on pages 34–43 and 44–53 respectively. The sequencing of each of these plans is the same, regardless of the floor level.

■ Phase I

The first phase of drawing the floor plan requires a tremendous amount of work. The goal during this phase is to get as much of the general construction information as possible drawn onto the sheet. This will enable other sheets in the set of construction documents to be started. It will also provide a basis for beginning more detailed conversations with the project consultants. Structural consultants will be particularly interested in the spans of major structural members as well as the locations of columns. Mechanical consultants will be interested in such items as glass locations, plumbing stacks, and final building orientation.

The Phase I drawing shows the earliest stage of this information. The drawing requires that certain assumptions be made. For the purposes of this book, all of the major items drafted in Phase I have been assumed to represent decisions that were made previously in the design process. Locations of entrances, vertical transportation, toilet rooms, and so forth are taken as given. Compliance with the required codes and regulations is also taken as given.

Although you would not start the partition types or wall sections for the document set during Phase I, assumptions are often made about the construction techniques that will be used for interior partitions and for exterior walls. The example in this book assumes that the exterior wall is constructed with 3⅝" brick, a 1" air space, ½" sheathing, a 6" structural steel stud, and ⅝" gypsum board.

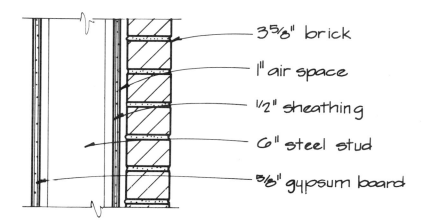

3⅝" brick

1" air space

½" sheathing

6" steel stud

⅝" gypsum board

Assumptions have also been made about the location of the exterior wall with relation to the column centerlines. A small amount of contingency space has been left that will allow the columns to change size during refined structural calculations. It is not uncommon in documentation to have to revise column sizes to reflect the addition of items that were not previously located on the drawings, such as a rooftop mechanical unit. In these cases, if the exterior of the wall has been located too tight to the column, a substantial amount of redrawing would have to occur to accommodate the new sizes of the structure. Thus, providing a contingency space may save time in later redrawing. In assumptions about the size of interior partitions, an inch or two is not critical, at this scale, to the graphic quality of the document. In order to have some starting point, however, toilet-room partitions have been drawn here with 6" metal studs, toilet chases as being 1'-6" wide, and all other interior partitions with 3⅝" metal studs.

From a sequencing perspective, it is best first to draw the column centerlines and label the column bubbles when drafting these plans. In so doing, you will establish a reference system that can be used on all other drawings within the set. Next, draft all major dimensions and reference them to the column centerlines, and then draft the preliminary structure. Sizes for structural members can be obtained from the structural consultant or from estimates that you can prepare based on guideline information available from the appropriate trades. Though these initial sizes may change, any revisions will probably be minor and not require any redrafting because of the small scale of the drawings.

The next items you should draft are the exterior walls and the interior partitions. Information on the location of these walls should be available from the design phase of the project. Finally, you should give the drawing its title and scale and properly fill in the title block information.

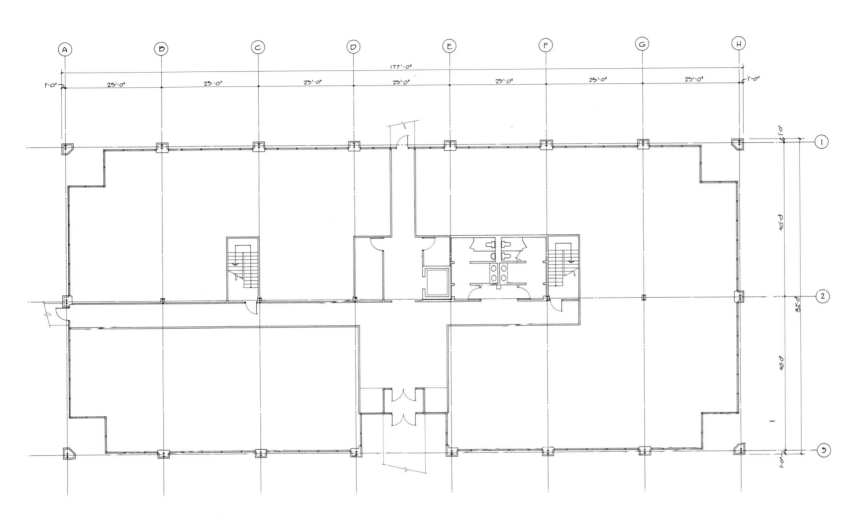

FIRST LEVEL FLOOR PLAN
0 1   8   16

A
SPECULATIVE
OFFICE
BUILDING
in
DUGONE COUNTY
for

NICHOLAS
PROPERTIES

GENW, PC.
architect

BUILDINGS R US
engineers

ISSUE:

DATE:

FIRST LEVEL
FLOOR PLAN

A-2

■ Phase II

The second phase of the floor plans documentation reflects the addition of cross-referencing. Building elevations, building sections, wall sections, and enlarged plans are all indicated and referenced. It is important to begin cross-referencing the set of construction documents as early as possible. This helps to tie the set together and thus avoid confusion. Strategies for locating where sections should be cut and which elevations should be drawn are discussed in the appropriate chapters.

More detailed dimensions are added to the drawings at this stage. Note that there will now be three dimension strings on the perimeter of the building. The outermost string gives the overall building dimensions, the middle string the structural bay spaces, and the inner string the dimensions of surface articulation.

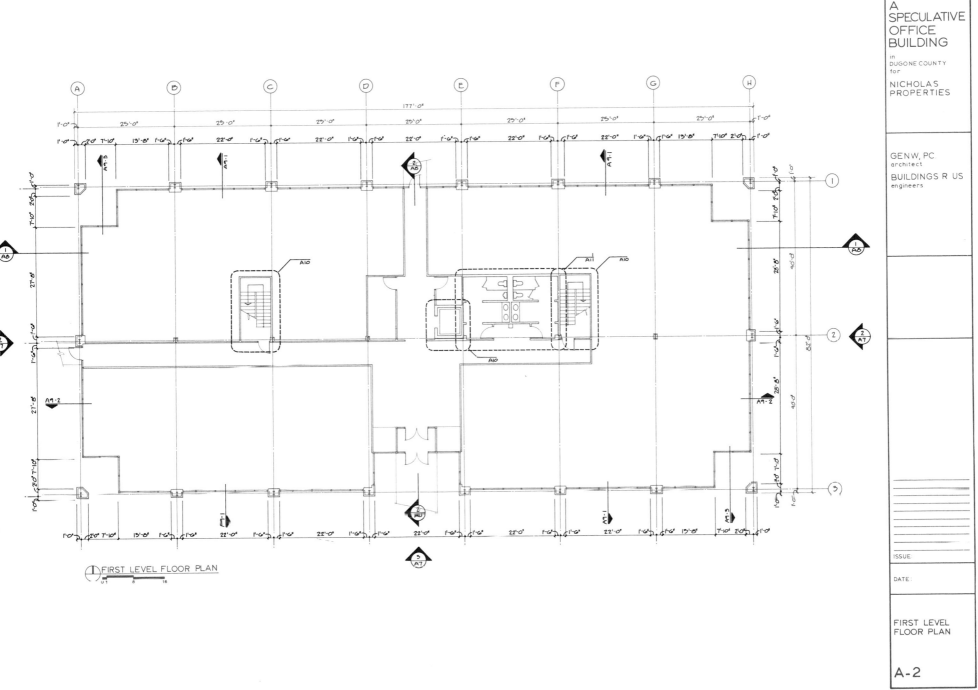

FIRST LEVEL FLOOR PLAN

A
SPECULATIVE
OFFICE
BUILDING
in
DUGONE COUNTY
for
NICHOLAS
PROPERTIES

GENW, PC
architect

BUILDINGS R US
engineers

ISSUE:

DATE:

FIRST LEVEL
FLOOR PLAN

A-2

■ Phase III

During the third phase room names and numbers are added to the document and doors are given their reference numbers. This allows the schedules to be developed (see Chapter II). During phase three you should also be developing many of the details for the detail book. Partitions types, which you should be developing at this point in the process, should have their references added to the plan during this phase along with other miscellaneous details.

Phase III is also an appropriate time to refine building features that might have been altered or added due to more detailed engineering work. Locations of transformers, telephone boards, electric panels, and so forth should be added and cross referenced. When you draw a feature such as a telephone board, it is appropriate to reference the proper engineering discipline with a note such as, "Telephone Board—Reference Electrical."

Finally, detailed dimensions are added to the drawings. These dimensions should locate all interior features. Note that areas that will be drafted as enlarged plans are dimensioned only on their perimeters. More detailed dimensions for these areas will be included on the enlarged plans. Also note that dimension strings consistently tie into column centerlines.

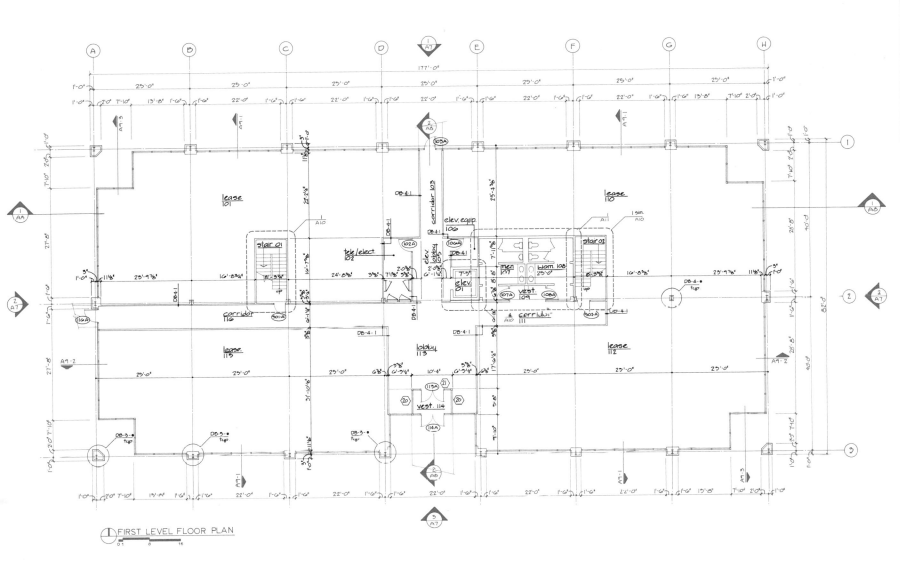

FIRST LEVEL FLOOR PLAN

A
SPECULATIVE
OFFICE
BUILDING
in
DUGONE COUNTY
for

NICHOLAS
PROPERTIES

GENW, PC
architect

BUILDINGS R US
engineers

ISSUE

DATE:

FIRST LEVEL
FLOOR PLAN

A-2

■ Phase IV

The final phase of the floor plan documentation reflects the addition of material indications. Although material indications are not essential in a set of construction documents, their inclusion is helpful and makes the drawings easier for others to understand. More important during this phase is the addition of miscellaneous notes. Frequently you will have wanted to include an item in the documents, but will not have had time to draw the item. In these cases it is important to at least note the item. In so doing you will have better assurance that the item will not be overlooked during the bid process of the project.

It is also important to check your work at this phase of the documentation. Verify all cross references, detail references, and dimension strings. It is far better to catch mistakes at this point in a project than after a set of documents has gone to bid.

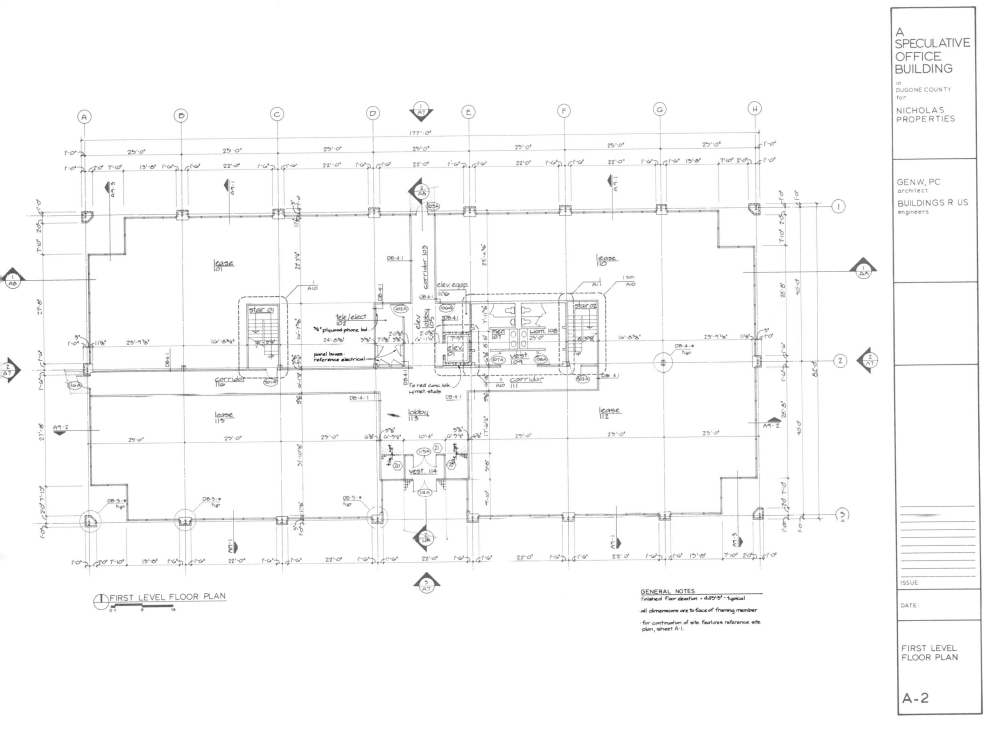

A
SPECULATIVE
OFFICE
BUILDING
in
DUGONE COUNTY
for

NICHOLAS
PROPERTIES

GENW, PC
architect

BUILDINGS R US
engineers

ISSUE

DATE:

FIRST LEVEL
FLOOR PLAN

A-2

GENERAL NOTES

· finished floor elevation = 445'-5" - typical

· all dimensions are to face of framing member

· for continuation of site features reference site plan, sheet A-1.

FIRST LEVEL FLOOR PLAN

■ The Completed First Level Floor Plan

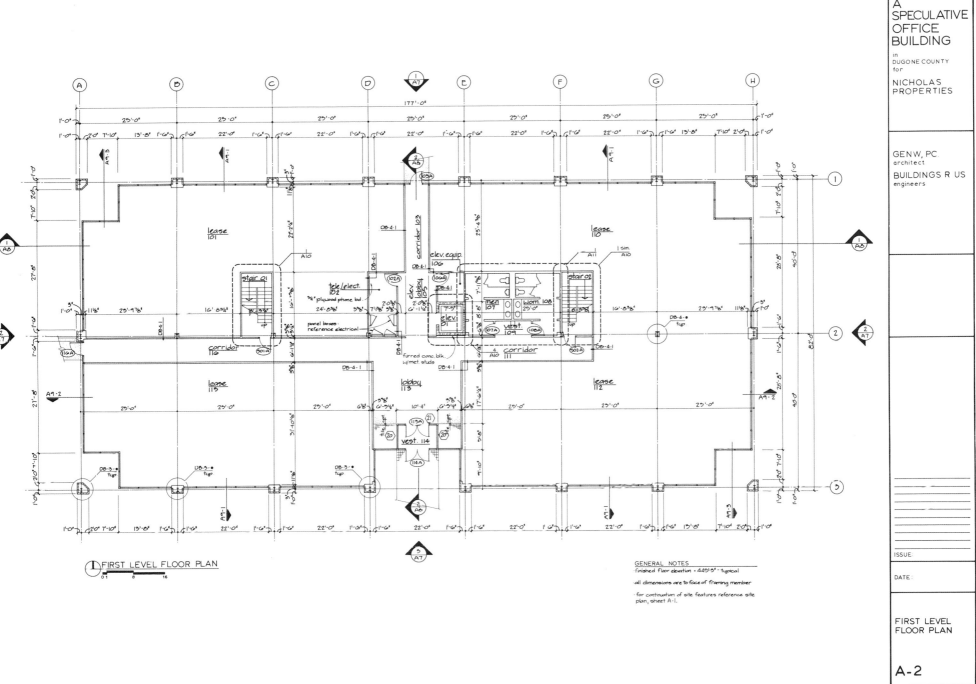

FIRST LEVEL FLOOR PLAN

A
SPECULATIVE
OFFICE
BUILDING
in
DUGONE COUNTY
for

NICHOLAS
PROPERTIES

GENW, PC.
architect

BUILDINGS R US
engineers

ISSUE:

DATE:

FIRST LEVEL
FLOOR PLAN

A-2

GENERAL NOTES
· finished floor elevation = 445'-5" = typical
· all dimensions are to face of framing member
· for continuation of site features reference site
plan, sheet A-1.

lease 101
lease 110
stair 01
stair 02
tele./elect. 102
elev. equip. 106
elev. lobby 105
men 107
wom. 108
elev. 01
vest. 109
corridor 116
corridor 111
lease 115
lobby 113
lease 112
vest. 114

■ **Phase I**

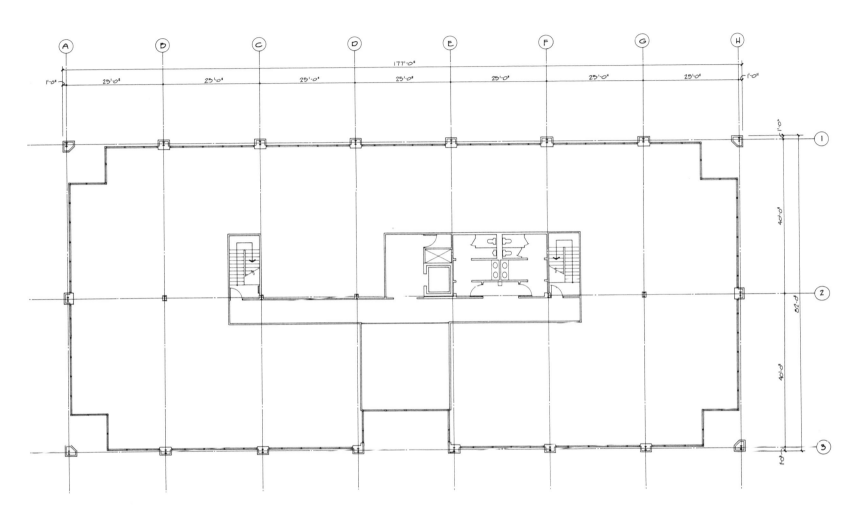

① SECOND LEVEL FLOOR PLAN
0 1   8   16

A
SPECULATIVE
OFFICE
BUILDING
in
DUGONE COUNTY
for

NICHOLAS
PROPERTIES

GEN W, PC
architect

BUILDINGS R US
engineers

ISSUE:

DATE:

SECOND LEVEL
FLOOR PLAN

A-3

45

■ Phase II

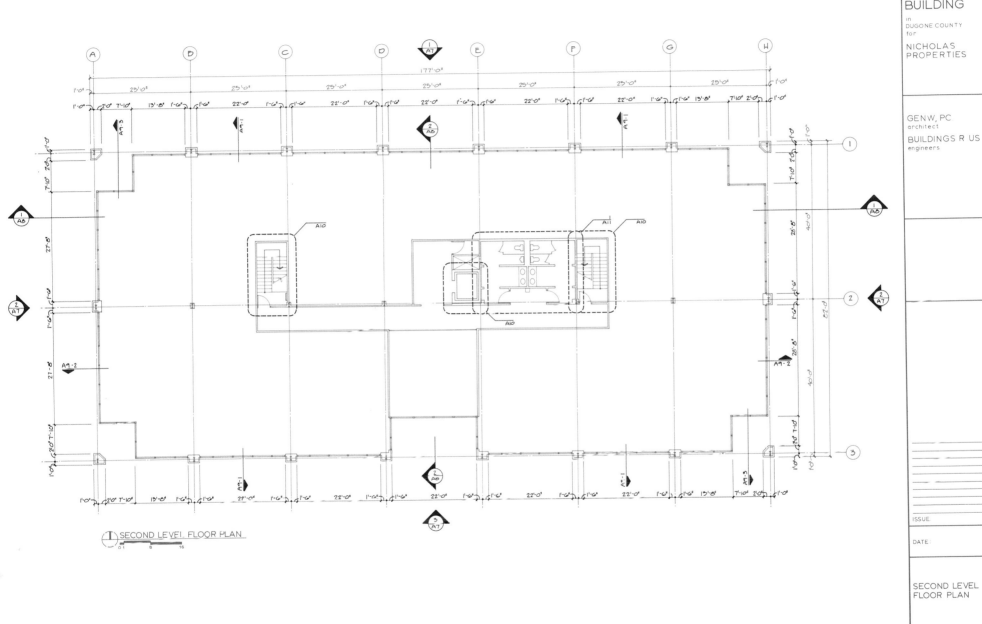

SECOND LEVEL FLOOR PLAN

A
SPECULATIVE
OFFICE
BUILDING
in
DUGONE COUNTY
for
NICHOLAS
PROPERTIES

GEN.W, PC
architect

BUILDINGS R US
engineers

ISSUE

DATE:

SECOND LEVEL
FLOOR PLAN

A-3

■ **Phase III**

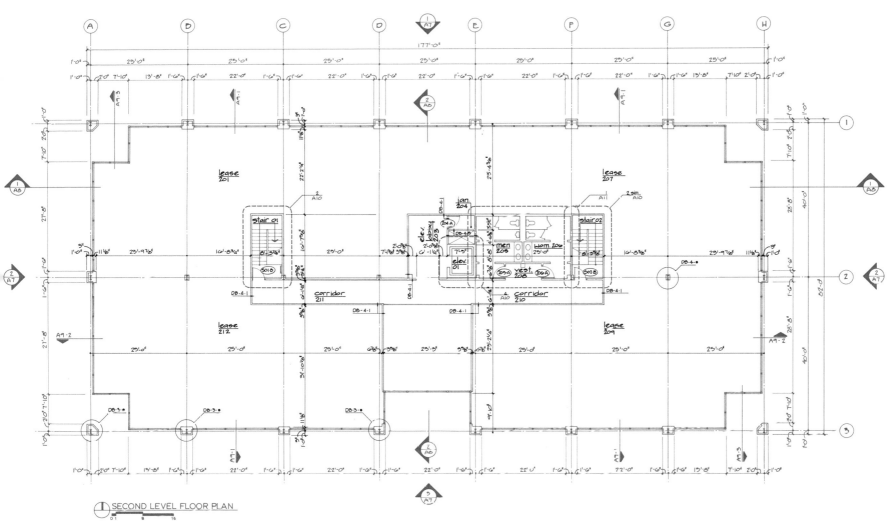

① SECOND LEVEL FLOOR PLAN

A
SPECULATIVE
OFFICE
BUILDING
in
DUGONE COUNTY
for

NICHOLAS
PROPERTIES

GENW, PC
architect

BUILDINGS R US
engineers

ISSUE:

DATE:

SECOND LEVEL
FLOOR PLAN

A-3

■ Phase IV

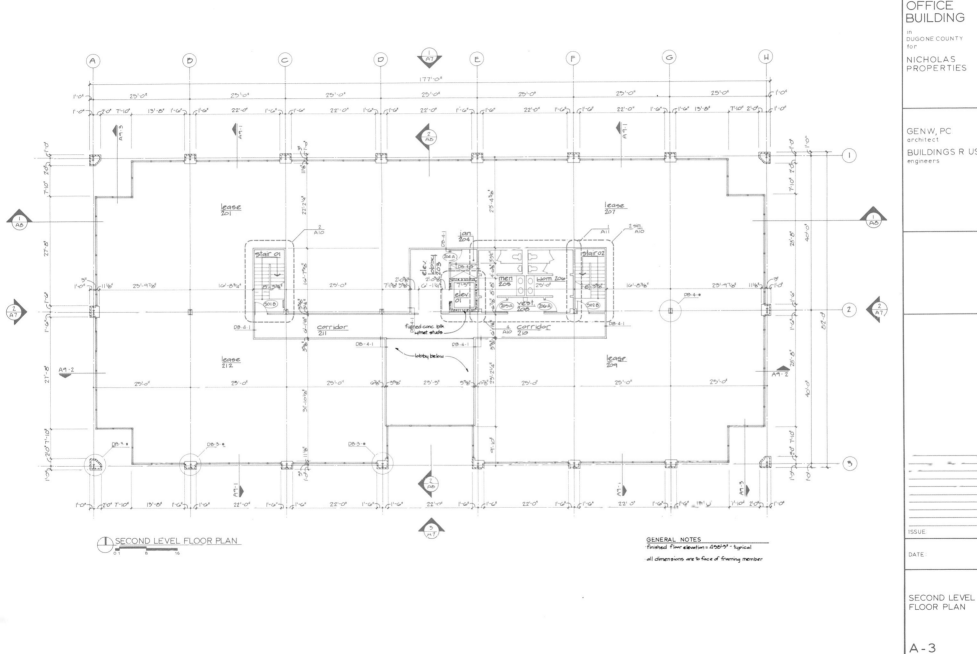

SECOND LEVEL FLOOR PLAN

GENERAL NOTES

finished floor elevation = 450'-3" - typical

all dimensions are to face of framing member

A
SPECULATIVE
OFFICE
BUILDING
in
DUGONE COUNTY
for
NICHOLAS
PROPERTIES

GEN W, PC
architect

BUILDINGS R US
engineers

ISSUE

DATE:

SECOND LEVEL
FLOOR PLAN

A-3

The Completed Second Level Floor Plan

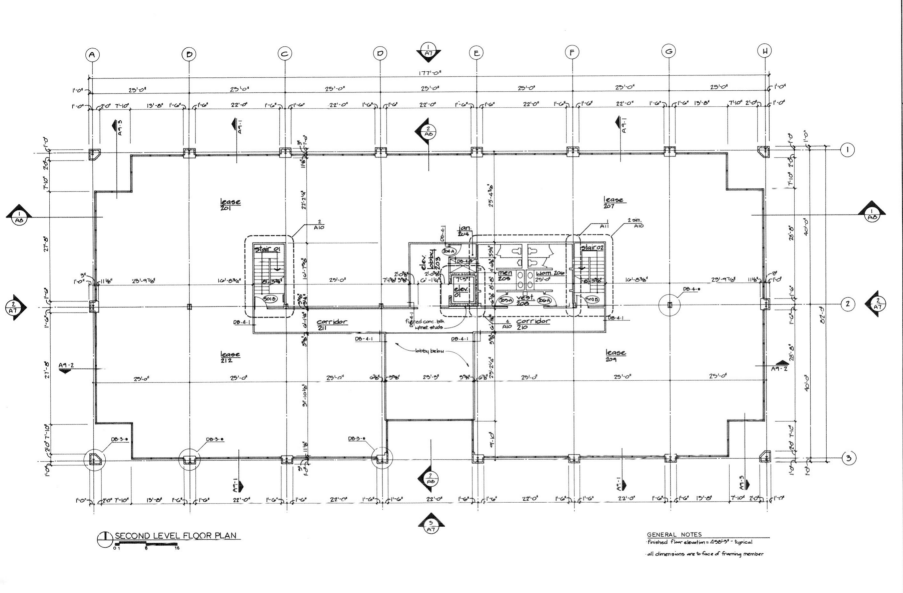

SECOND LEVEL FLOOR PLAN

A
SPECULATIVE
OFFICE
BUILDING

in
DUGONE COUNTY
for

NICHOLAS
PROPERTIES

GENW, PC.
architect

BUILDINGS R US
engineers

ISSUE:

DATE:

SECOND LEVEL
FLOOR PLAN

A-3

GENERAL NOTES
- finished floor elevation = 458'-3" - typical
- all dimensions are to face of framing member

lease 201

lease 207

lease 212

lease 209

stair 01

stair 02

corridor 211

corridor 210

elev. lobby 203

jan. 204

men 205

wom. 206

vest. 208

elev. 01

lobby below

177'-0"

4 Roof Plans

Roof plans are generally started early in the process of construction documentation. This is not so much because of the information they provide for other architectural documents, but for the information they provide for engineering consultants.

■ General Information

The mechanical consultant will want to know the locations of roof drains and/or roof scuppers, as well as the acceptable locations for fan units, vent stacks, and so forth in terms of architectural design. If the use of rooftop mechanical units is planned, the mechanical consultant will also want to know about their acceptable locations, as well as the characteristics of the areas around these locations.

The structural consultant will be concerned with the locations of roof drains, which will dictate the slopes of the roof. These slopes must be designed early into the construction documentation process so that the elevations of structural members can be determined. The structural consultant will also want to know the locations of anticipated mechanical equipment on the roof. Of particular concern will be whether or not rooftop mechanical units will be used for the building. The weight of these units can have a major impact on the design of the structure of the entire building. Therefore, their location should be determined as soon as possible.

As with the site plan, when you are preparing the roof plan, you should imagine being above the building, looking down on the roof. All of the architectural and engineering features located on the roof will be visible. In addition, lines are drawn to indicate where the slopes of the roof are occurring.

There are numerous methods that can be used to calculate the slope of the roof. In order to do these calculations, you must first decide which roofing system you will be using for the building. An inverted roof membrane assembly has one set of requirements for how steep the slope of the roof should be, while a built-up roofing system has another. The recommended slopes for the different roof systems is readily available in the manufacturer's literature. This book uses a built-up roofing system and a minimum roof slope of ⅛" per foot.

If you are using roof drains do not expect a single drain to drain an entire roof. The amount of roof area that a drain can handle will depend upon the size of the drain itself along with the geographic location of the project. Remember that roof drain leaders must come down inside the building and that an extremely large leader may pose problems for the design of the interior. Also remember that on a building with a parapet it is typical to have an overflow roof drain located next to the main drain. The overflow drain, which is raised slightly in elevation above the main drain, will have a leader of the same size as the main leader, and it too will need to be accommodated on the interior of the building. In lieu of an overflow roof drain, you can provide scuppers in the exterior parapets.

Roof plans should be drawn at the same scale as floor plans. This provides consistency in the construction documents. It also helps to save time in drawing, as the outline of the roof as well as the column centerlines can be traced from the floor plan.

When positioning the roof plan on the sheet, you should put it in the same location as the floor plans. Again, this helps the documents to be consistent. If, however, this positioning is not possible, you should still follow the general convention of the profession by having the north arrow pointing up or to the right-hand side of the sheet.

In dimensioning the roof plan, I prefer to use framing dimensions. This system, which is described in Chapter 3, is appropriate for the nature of the items that will need to be located on the roof and consistent with the sequence of construction.

■ Appropriate Notes and Symbols

All of the different elevations of the roof should be clearly labeled. These elevations are typically shown as spot elevations, which are indicated by an angular leader terminating with a heavy dot. The dot represents the point being referenced. All peaks and valleys, as well as all roof drains, should be given spot elevations.

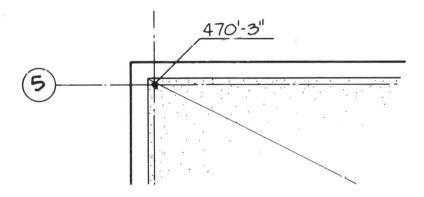

Dimensions should be in strings that are continuous when possible. Because so little on a roof plan will actually require a dimension, short strings are acceptable. When a dimension string intersects a column centerline, that intersection should be marked with a dot.

When a dimension string intersects any other feature, you should mark that intersection with a slash drawn at a 45-degree angle. The slash for vertical dimensions should slope from left to right; the slope for horizontal dimensions from right to left.

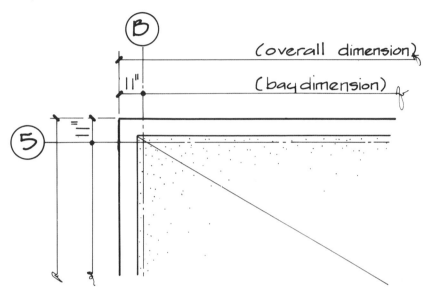

All roof drains should be shown on the roof plan. The note "RD" should be placed next to any circle that is intended to represent a drain.

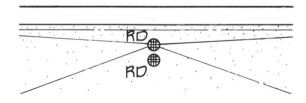

Column centerlines and column designation bubbles should be drafted in such a way that the centerline runs through the entire roof plan. Drawn as a series of long lines and single dashes, the column centerlines form the basic reference point for all dimension lines. The size of the centerline bubble should be appropriate for the designation to be labeled within it. All bubbles should be the same size, and should be located at the top of the roof plan for horizontal dimensions and to the right-hand side of the roof plan for vertical dimensions. Bubbles should be drafted several inches from the roof plan to allow space for dimension lines.

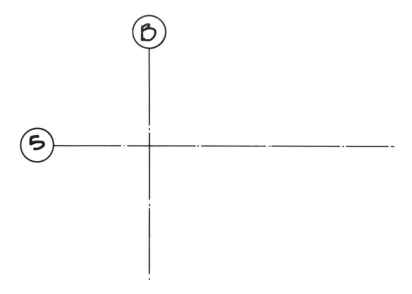

Cross-referencing cuts—wall sections. The arrow symbol shown below refers to a wall section that is located on another sheet within the set of construction documents. Underneath the arrow is a number to help locate the section. The first number refers to the sheet number, while the second number refers to the particular drawing on the sheet. The size of the arrowhead is not critical, although once a size has been selected, it should be held constant for all of the drawings. A good system for drawing arrows is to make the bottom of the arrow a minimum of ⅜″ and to draw the sides with the 30-degree side of a 30/60 triangle.

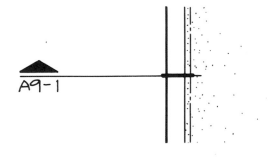

Cross-referencing cuts—building section. This next symbol refers to a building section that is located on another sheet within the set of construction documents. The bottom number refers to the sheet number, while the top number refers to the particular drawing on the sheet. The size of the circle should be such that it can easily contain the information that is labeled inside of it. Once a size is selected, all circles should be consistent and adhere to the standard.

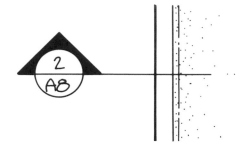

Other features that should be shown on the roof plan might include special paving blocks for foot traffic on the roof, mechanical fans, vents, penthouse equipment, skylights, screens, and roof hatches. Details would include parapet conditions, flashing conditions, roof drains, and scuppers. All details should be referenced to the detail book by either a cut arrow with a reference number or by a reference circle with a reference number.

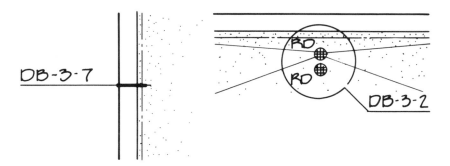

All materials should be properly indicated in accordance with the standards described in Chapter 1.

■ Sequence of the Documentation Procedure

The roof plan is drafted in three phases.

■ Phase I

The goal of the first phase of the preparation of any set of construction documents is to get as much information as possible shown on the drawings so that, in an office or team situation, others can begin to use them. It should be remembered that it is not possible to do the entire drawing in the first phase. Many of the documents in the drawing set must be performed concurrently. You also need time to receive consultant feedback. This process is particularly evident when drawing the roof plan. Because of this, only the most basic information can be presented during the first phase of this drawing.

As with the floor plans, the column centerlines and column bubbles should be drafted and labeled first. Major dimensions should be included and referenced to the centerlines. After these have been drafted, the building perimeter can be added.

The building perimeter should be drawn as a double line, which is intended to indicate a thickness of the roof parapet. Roof parapets may or may not be required by the building code. The example in this book includes a building parapet; the assumption has also been made that the parapet will have a construction that is similar to the wall below it. Thus the construction estimate includes 3⅝" brick, a 1" air space, ½" sheathing, 6" structural steel studs, and ¾" exterior grade plywood with appropriate flashing.

Rooftop features should be drawn next, although all features may not be known at this time. In the sample drawing, it has been known from the design phase that there will be four skylights over the main lobby and that a roof hatch will be required. Finally, the drawing should be given its title and scale, and the title block should be filled in properly.

The roof plan is now ready to give to the mechanical consultant, who can then locate any needed rooftop features. In the example shown, the assumption has been made that the building will have a rooftop mechanical unit. It is important to locate this unit as early as possible so that roof drains can be located, roof slopes calculated, and structural coordination initiated during Phase II.

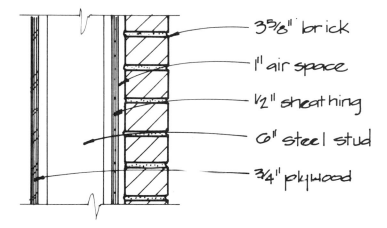

3⅝" brick

1" air space

½" sheathing

6" steel stud

¾" plywood

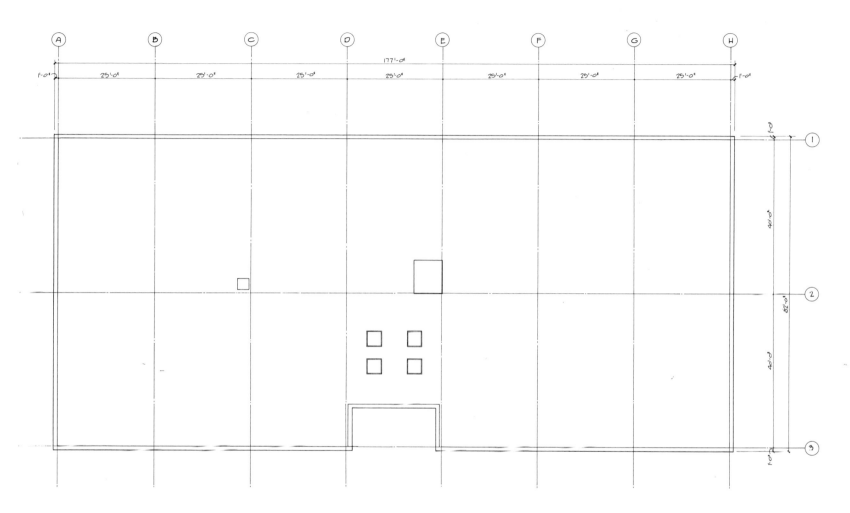

A
SPECULATIVE
OFFICE
BUILDING
in
DUGONE COUNTY
for

NICHOLAS
PROPERTIES

GENW, PC.
architect

BUILDINGS R US
engineers

ISSUE:

DATE:

ROOF PLAN

A-4

A
B
C
D
E
F
G
H

177'-0"

1'-0"   25'-0"   25'-0"   25'-0"   25'-0"   25'-0"   25'-0"   25'-0"   1'-0"

1'-0"

40'-0"

82'-0"

40'-0"

1'-0"

1

2

3

1 ROOF PLAN

0 1   8   16

■ Phase II

The sample second phase of the roof plan documentation shows that the rooftop mechanical equipment has been located. Its location is indicated by a mechanical curb, which has been noted and referenced to the detail book. The roof drains have also been located and the roof slopes have been calculated. Note that roof drains have not been located on the tops of column centerlines, but rather are situated slightly to their sides. This is because the roof drain cannot sit on top of the joist or beam that would be located along the centerline.

The slopes of the roof are indicated with spot elevations. When deciding whether or not a particular point should receive a spot elevation, your philosophy should always be that it is better to have too many elevations referenced than to have too few. Arrows are also drawn at this stage to indicate graphically the general direction of the flows.

Note that when a portion of the roof that is sloping down to a drain comes to a penetration such as a roof hatch or mechanical curb, a "cricketed" area is built up on the uphill side of the penetration. This is done to direct water away from the edge of the penetration. However, not all roofing systems will require crickets. You should consult the manufacturer's literature to see if crickets are needed with the roof system you are using.

Dimensions are added to the document in this phase in order to locate rooftop features. Miscellaneous notes and additional rooftop projections are also drafted. At this level of development, the roof plan can be given to the structural consultant for final top of steel elevations and locations of mechanical equipment.

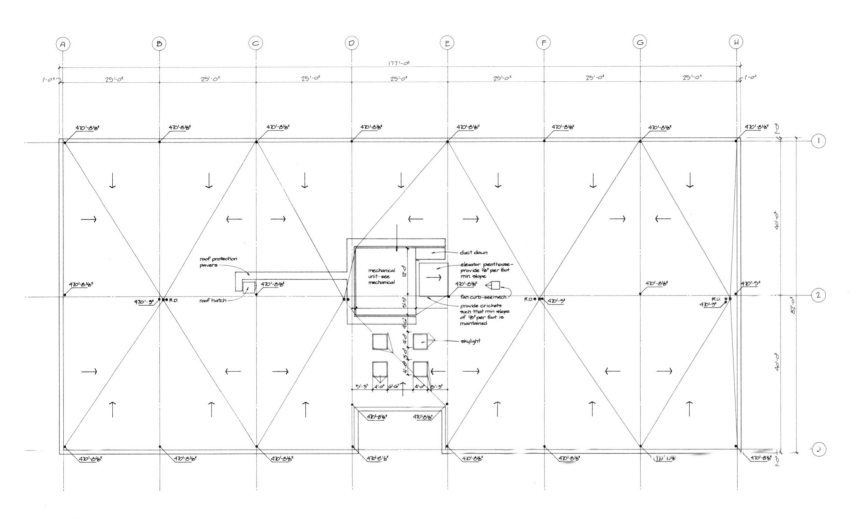

A
SPECULATIVE
OFFICE
BUILDING
in
DUGONE COUNTY
for

NICHOLAS
PROPERTIES

GEN W, PC
architect

BUILDINGS R US
engineers

ISSUE

DATE:

ROOF PLAN

A-4

ROOF PLAN

177'-0"

1'-0" 25'-0" 25'-0" 25'-0" 25'-0" 25'-0" 25'-0" 25'-0" 1'-0"

470'-8⅛" 470'-8⅛" 470'-8⅛" 470'-8⅛" 470'-8⅛" 470'-8⅛" 470'-8⅛" 470'-8⅛"

roof protection pavers

mechanical unit - see mechanical

duct down

elevator penthouse - provide ⅛" per foot min. slope

470'-8⅛"

fan curb - see mech. provide crickets such that min. slope of ⅛" per foot is maintained

roof hatch

470'-3" R.O.

R.O. 470'-3"

R.O. 470'-3"

470'-5"

skylight

5'-3" 4'-0" 6'-6" 4'-0" 5'-3"

470'-8⅛" 470'-8⅛"

470'-8⅛" 470'-8⅛" 470'-8⅛" 470'-8⅛" 470'-8⅛" 470'-8⅛" 470'-8⅛" 470'-8⅛"

A B C D E F G H

1 2 J

40'-0" 40'-0" 82'-0"

■ Phase III

Cross-referencing is added in the third phase of the roof plan documentation. Building sections, wall sections, and details are indicated and referenced. Details that have been referenced should be drawn and added to the detail book.

Miscellaneous notes are also added to the drawing. As has been mentioned previously, it is critical that all features be adequately noted if they are not drafted. Material indications are also added to the drawing. These indications are very easy to draw in a roof plan and help to clarify the roofing indications. If time were critical, however, these indications could be deleted.

The last step in drafting the roof plan is to verify all of the information on the sheet. Particularly critical for the roof is to check all of the slopes to the roof drains. If ⅛″ fall per foot is not achieved, there will be a strong potential for ponding on the roof. Because roof leaks are potential liability problems, it is important that no unplanned ponding take place.

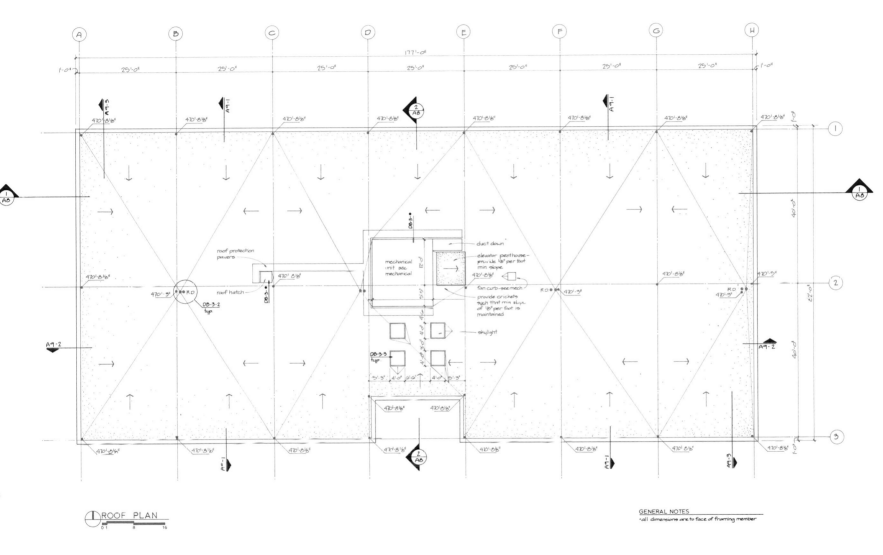

ROOF PLAN

GENERAL NOTES
·all dimensions are to face of framing member

A
SPECULATIVE
OFFICE
BUILDING
in
DUGONE COUNTY
for

NICHOLAS
PROPERTIES

GENW, PC
architect

BUILDINGS R US
engineers

ISSUE

DATE

ROOF PLAN

A-4

The Completed Roof Plan

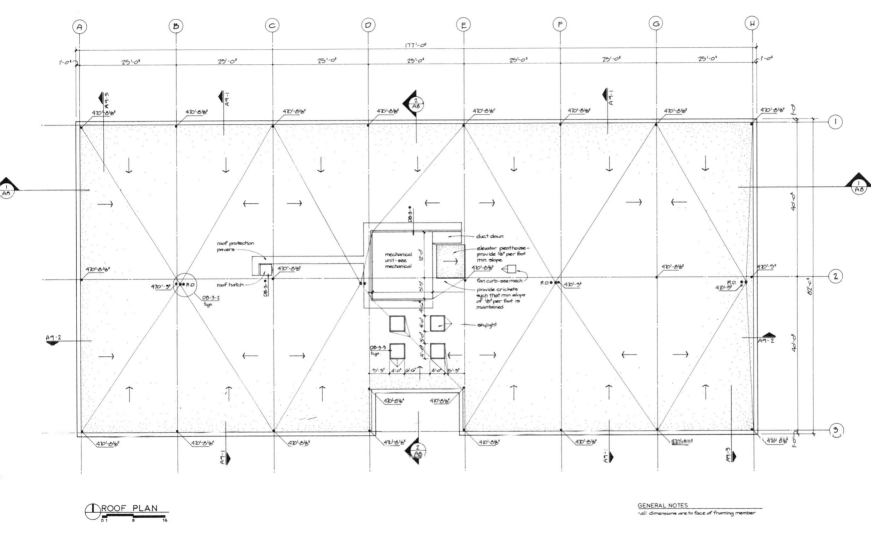

ROOF PLAN

GENERAL NOTES
·all dimensions are to face of framing member

A
SPECULATIVE
OFFICE
BUILDING
in
DUGONE COUNTY
for
NICHOLAS
PROPERTIES

GEN.W, P.C.
architect

BUILDINGS R US
engineers

ISSUE:

DATE:

ROOF PLAN

A-4

5 Reflected Ceiling Plans

Reflected ceiling plans are typically started one-third to one-half of the way through the preparation of the set of construction documents. Their purpose is to convey to the contractor exactly how the ceiling is supposed to look.

■ General Information

Items that will be located on reflected ceiling plans include lighting, air devices, material indications, and soffits. Some architects will also locate sprinkler heads on the drawing. Although a sprinkler system is not shown in the documentation for this book, one could easily be added to the drawings. If this were done, the locations of the sprinkler heads would need to be carefully considered. Within certain constraints, these heads can be positioned to contribute to a pleasing composition of ceiling elements. Aligning heads with other elements of the ceiling so that an axial treatment is achieved is recommended. You should also be aware that in many cases the decision of whether or not to include a sprinkler system in a building will be based on information from the building code as well as preliminary pricing. Frequently it is more cost-effective to install a sprinkler system than it is to meet the requirements of the code that will be enforced in the absence of a sprinkler system.

When drafting a reflected ceiling plan, you should imagine that you are lying down on the floor of a room and looking up at the ceiling. What you see is what is drawn. In addition to these ceiling features, there are also a number of miscellaneous items that can be shown on the plan. Items such as penetrations through partitions that occur above the ceiling plane, as well as partition head conditions, can be indicated graphically and noted.

Reflected ceiling plans should be drawn at the same scale as the floor plans. This provides consistency in the construction documents. It also helps to save time in drafting, as the basic plan as well as the column centerlines can be traced from the floor plan.

When locating the reflected ceiling plan on the sheet, it is good practice to try to situate it in the same location as the floor plans. This reinforces consistency between the documents. If, however, this is not possible, you should follow the general convention of the profession by having the north arrow pointing up or to the right-hand side of the sheet. "Actual" dimensions have been used in this book for the reflected ceiling plans. This system, which is described in Chapter 3, is appropriate primarily because of the sequence of construction. When the ceiling is installed, it is typical for the interior partitions and exterior walls to be in place. Frequently, they have already been given their initial finish treatment. The actual system of dimensioning takes this occurrence into account by relying on finish rather than framing dimensions.

The first step in preparing the reflected ceiling plan is to decide on the types and locations of ceiling materials to be used. The two most common systems used today are gypsum board ceilings supported by suspended metal grillage, and suspended acoustical ceilings. Suspended acoustical ceilings provide good flexibility, economy, and ease of maintenance. They also make it easy to access items that are located above the ceiling plane. Gypsum board ceilings can provide more elegant and, in some cases, more durable ceilings. They are, however, more expensive. It is also much more difficult to service items that are located above them. Gypsum board ceilings should always have metal access panels installed in them to help solve this potential problem.

In laying out a suspended acoustical ceiling there are certain logical guidelines that you should follow, regardless of the project type. For example, it is important to be aware of the construction of the interior partition heads at the ceiling. When partitions do not penetrate the ceiling plane, there is no need to stop the grid at the partition head. This allows the ceiling contractor to construct large areas of the ceiling in a shorter period of time than if there were numerous smaller areas to be laid out. Thus, a cost savings can be realized for the project. When partitions break the ceiling plane and run to the structure above, the ceiling grid will have to terminate at either side of the partition. Although this will mean increased costs, it will also provide greater security between spaces, as well as increased sound isolation. In terms of sequencing your work on the documents, it is advisable to decide which partitions should run to the structure above before laying out the suspended acoustical ceiling grid. This decision will be based on design intent as well as on requirements for fire separations that might be called for in the building code.

You should also think about the lighting and air distribution for a space when laying out the ceiling grid. In a small office where the location of a desk is fairly obvious, it will be appropriate to locate the ceiling grid so that a lighting fixture can be placed over and slightly in front of the desk. In larger offices, the placement of the grid may help to eliminate dark spots by ensuring that a lighting fixture will fit into any part of the plan.

Finally, you need to lay out the ceiling grid so that there are equal distances on each side of the space where the grid meets a hard edge, such as an exterior wall or a partition that penetrates the ceiling plane. Care should be taken to reduce the number of ceiling tiles that will need to be cut as thin slivers.

Obviously there will be compromises in grid configuration. You should seek, however, to maximize the positives and minimize the negatives with the layout.

The next concern in the production of the reflected ceiling plan deals with the number and locations of lighting fixtures. Fluorescent lighting fixtures are one of the more common types of lighting being used today. They have a low operating cost, produce little heat, and provide an even light. The number of fixtures that will be required for a given space will depend upon the type of fixture that is selected, as well as client preference. Photometrics are available in manufacturer's literature to aid in fixture layout.

Incandescent lighting fixtures can have a more elegant effect than fluorescent fixtures. They are particularly appropriate for accent lighting or special lighting (as in a reception area or conference room). However, because the lights generate substantial amounts of heat, a space that contains many incandescent fixtures will require more cooling than will a room with only fluorescent fixtures.

When laying out lighting fixtures for gypsum board ceilings, you should make sure that the fixtures are located dimensionally on the plan. By doing so, you will ensure that their placement is not only functional but also aesthetically pleasing.

After you have selected the ceiling systems and located the light fixtures, you should locate the air devices. Air devices will typically include supply and return air grills as well as special features such as exhaust fans. It is a good idea to place supply and return grills away from each other to ensure that the space will have proper ventilation. Aesthetics should also be considered when locating air devices. Aligning elements in the ceiling into rows or columns will help to provide a more uniform and professional result. In gypsum board ceilings, you should dimension the location of air devices to further ensure that they are not located haphazardly by the contractor.

■ Appropriate Notes and Symbols

All of the different ceiling heights should be noted. These heights are measured as the distance above the finished floor, and are labeled inside an ellipse. The size of the ellipse is not critical, but should be held constant for the entire set of documents. When the ceiling in a building primarily maintains the same elevation, the elevation can be listed as a general note with only the variations being noted on the reflected ceiling plan.

Any partition that goes to the structure above that will have a hole located in it (such as for a wall-mounted access panel) should have the opening size labeled next to a rectangle that has been drawn in scale to represent the size of the opening. If the location of the hole is critical, it should be tied dimensionally to a known object.

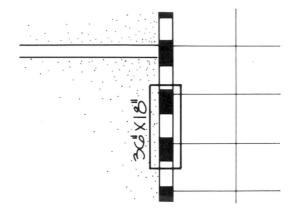

Dimensions should be in strings that are continuous when possible. Because so little in a reflected ceiling plan will actually require a dimension, short strings are acceptable. When a dimension string intersects a column centerline, the intersection should be marked with a dot. When a dimension string intersects any other feature, that intersection should be marked with a slash drawn at a 45-degree angle. This slash should slope left to right for vertical dimensions and from right to left for horizontal dimensions.

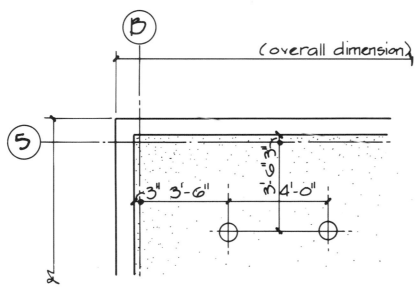

Column centerlines and column designation bubbles should be drafted in such a way that the centerline extends to within ½" of the edge of the reflected ceiling plan. All bubbles should be the same size and should be located at the top of the plan for the horizontal dimensions and to the right-hand side of the plan for the vertical dimensions. Bubbles should be drafted several inches away from the plan to allow space for dimension lines.

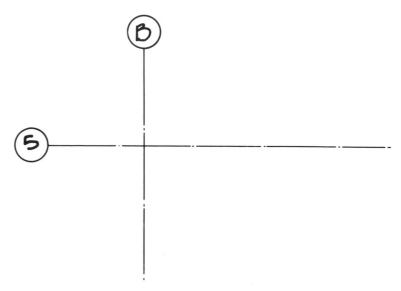

Partitions that do not penetrate the ceiling plane should be drawn as double lines that are not colored in with any pattern. Partitions that do penetrate the ceiling plane should be colored in with alternating bands of color.

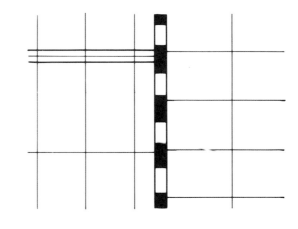

Doors into rooms should be drawn in lightly on the reflected ceiling plan. This is done to aid in locating the wall switches, which will frequently be situated immediately next to the door. The location of switches will be primarily a design function, although circuiting of lighting fixtures should be reviewed with the electrical consultant. Although switches do not have to be drawn, if they are they should be indicated by an "S" with a line through it.

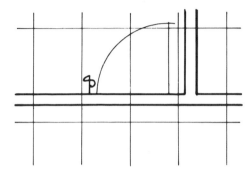

Control joints in gypsum board ceilings should be drafted as a thin double line with the note "CJ" located next to it. Frequently control joints will occur along known features such as column centerlines. In these instances, where locations are graphically clear, no dimensioning is required. Otherwise, control joints should be dimensioned with reference to a known feature to ensure that their locations will not be performed haphazardly. You should refer to gypsum board industry standards for the spacing of control joints.

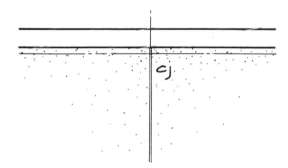

Fluorescent lighting fixtures (except "strip" fixtures) should be drawn to scale as rectangles on the reflected ceiling plan. A bold line weight should be used to ensure that the fixtures will stand out against the ceiling grid.

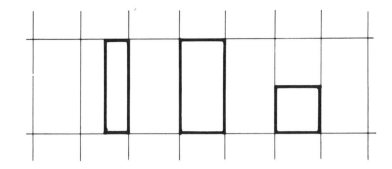

"Strip" fluorescent lighting fixtures should be drawn as a heavy elongated "I" shape. These fixtures are typically surface-mounted and have exposed tubes.

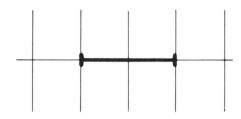

Exit lights should be drawn as a circle with a partially blackened "X" located within the circle.

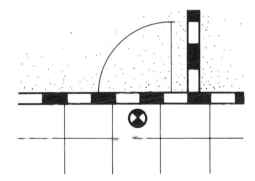

Incandescent lighting fixtures should be drawn as circles or squares, as appropriate for the unit selected. Standard downlights have nothing drawn in the interior of the symbol. Wall-washer (accent) lights are drawn with one half of the symbol blackened.

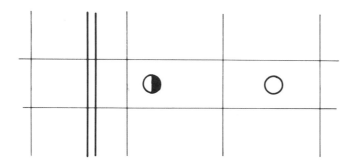

Sprinkler heads, when shown, should be indicated as small (¹⁄₁₆″) black dots.

Supply air devices should be drawn to scale as rectangles with an "X" drawn inside.

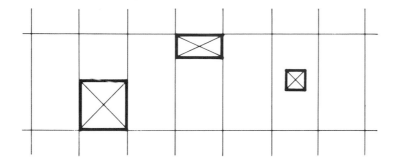

Return air devices should be drawn to scale as rectangles with a slash drawn inside.

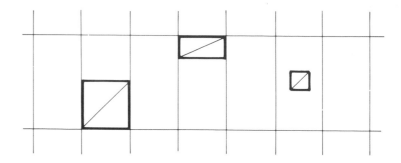

Other features that should be drawn on the reflected ceiling plan might include skylights, soffits, curtain tracks, and so forth. All architectural details should be referenced to the detail book by a cut arrow with a reference number.

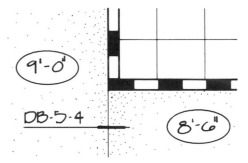

All materials should be properly indicated in accordance with the standards described in Chapter 1.

■ Sequence of the Documentation Procedure

Documents for both first and the second level plans are included as examples of reflected ceiling plans documentation on pages 72–79 and 80–87 respectively. The sequencing of each of these plans is the same, regardless of the floor level.

There are three phases in the preparation of the reflected ceiling plan. Because the first phase of general documentation is not used, this sequential description starts with Phase II.

Phase I
Not used.

■ Phase II

The initial drawing that is done for a reflected ceiling plan consists of tracing the exterior walls, interior partitions, and column centerlines from the floor plan. Doors and door swings should be traced lightly, and the head of the door should appear as a continuous part of the adjoining partition.

After this base has been drawn, you can then begin to indicate what types of ceiling systems are being used and where they are being located. Gypsum board ceilings will require no drawing at this stage of documentation. Suspended acoustical ceilings will need to have their ceiling grids drawn. Care should be taken to follow the guidelines described in this chapter when deciding on the grid configuration. In instances where there is not going to be a ceiling installed (such as in a mechanical room), the note, "Open to Structure Above" should be added to the proper space.

Soffits, which will typically be constructed with metal studs and gypsum board, should also be drawn at this stage of documentation.

After you properly fill in the sheet's title block and add the drawing title, the reflected ceiling plan will be ready to review with the engineering consultants. You should also review numbers and types of lights with the electrical consultant before you draw them onto the final document. Following your decision on lighting fixture locations, you should review the proper locations for air handling devices with the mechanical consultant.

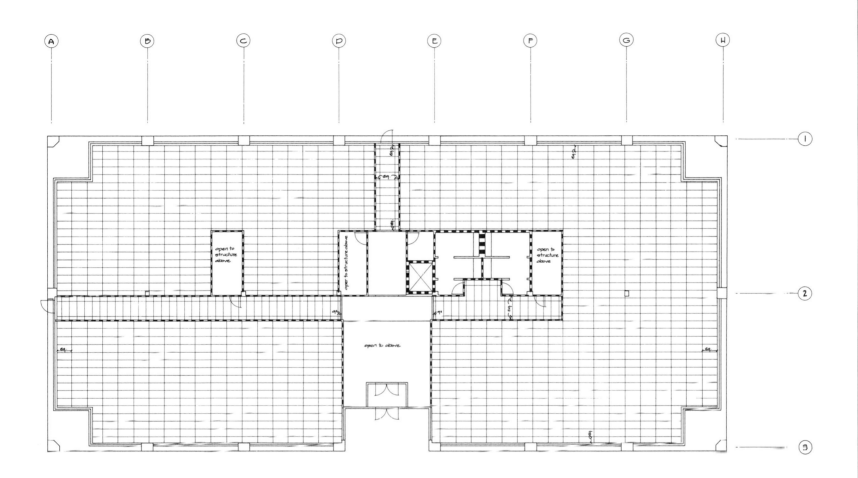

A
SPECULATIVE
OFFICE
BUILDING
in
DUGONE COUNTY
for
NICHOLAS
PROPERTIES

GEN W, PC
architect
BUILDINGS R US
engineers

ISSUE:

DATE:

FIRST LEVEL
REFLECTED
CEILING PLAN

A-5

Ⓐ   Ⓑ   Ⓒ   Ⓓ   Ⓔ   Ⓕ   Ⓖ   Ⓗ

①

②

③

open to
structure
above

open to structure above

open to
structure
above

open to above

① FIRST LEVEL REFLECTED CEILING PLAN
01   8   16

■ Phase III

In the third phase of the reflected ceiling plan documentation all lighting fixtures and air-handling devices are added. As mentioned, the location of these features depends on both function and design intent. Their final placement should be reviewed with the engineering consultants.

Lighting should be located before air-handling devices. This is because the exact location of lights is generally more critical than the exact location of air devices.

In the example, fixtures have been shown for the general lease area. When actual leasing is done, some of these fixtures will probably be relocated. Another option would have been to not install any light fixtures or ceiling tiles. In that case, light fixtures and ceiling tiles would be stockpiled and installed as needed by the new tenants.

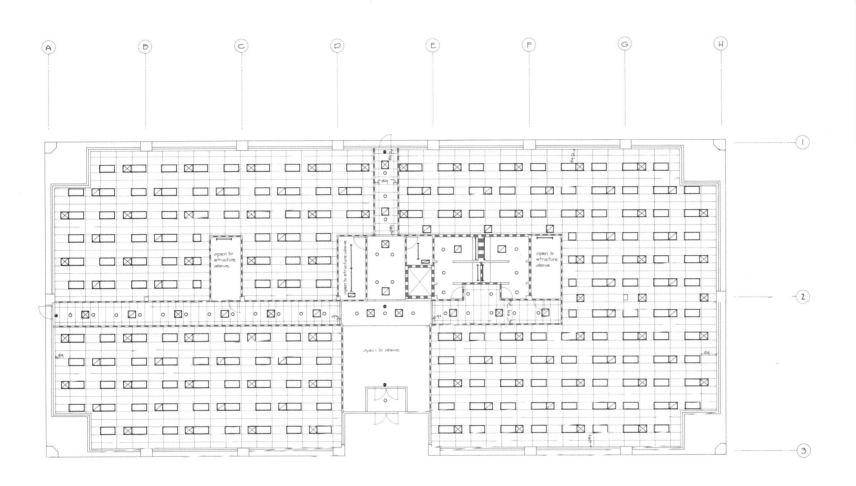

A B C D E F G H

1

open to
structure
above

open to
structure
above

open to
structure
above

2

open to above

3

① FIRST LEVEL REFLECTED CEILING PLAN

0 1   8   16

A
SPECULATIVE
OFFICE
BUILDING
in
DUGONE COUNTY
for

NICHOLAS
PROPERTIES

GENW, PC
architect

BUILDINGS R US
engineers

ISSUE:

DATE:

FIRST LEVEL
REFLECTED
CEILING PLAN

A-5

■ Phase IV

In the final phase of the reflected ceiling plan documentation all detail references are added. These details should be drawn and added to the detail book.

Miscellaneous notes are also added to the drawing at this stage. Although there are a limited number of detail items to be referenced on the reflected ceiling plans, any feature that has not been adequately detailed should be noted on the drawing to ensure its inclusion in the construction bid.

Material indications are also now added to the drawing. The primary indication required is for gypsum board ceilings. Because this is a relatively easy indication to draw, and because it helps to make the drawing more graphically concise, it is recommended that this indication be drawn, even if material indications have not been shown for some of the other documents. By adding indications to the drawing you will provide a good graphic clarification of the difference between a gypsum board ceiling and a ceiling that is open to the structure above.

All items located in gypsum board ceilings are located dimensionally. If an item is centered between two walls, it is acceptable to note the two halves as "equal" rather than to put in specific dimensions. Because the goal is to center the element, an actual dimension is not important. Use of the note "equal" also means that fewer revisions or chances for error will occur if minor dimensional modifications are required on the plan.

The most critical item to check on the reflected ceiling plan is the area between the bottom of the structure above and the top of the ceiling. The architect should make sure that the ductwork sizes that have been indicated by the mechanical consultant will actually fit into the space that has been provided. All of the ductwork cannot be squeezed down to a depth of 6" and a width of 15'-0". Many architects learn to do this check the hard way.

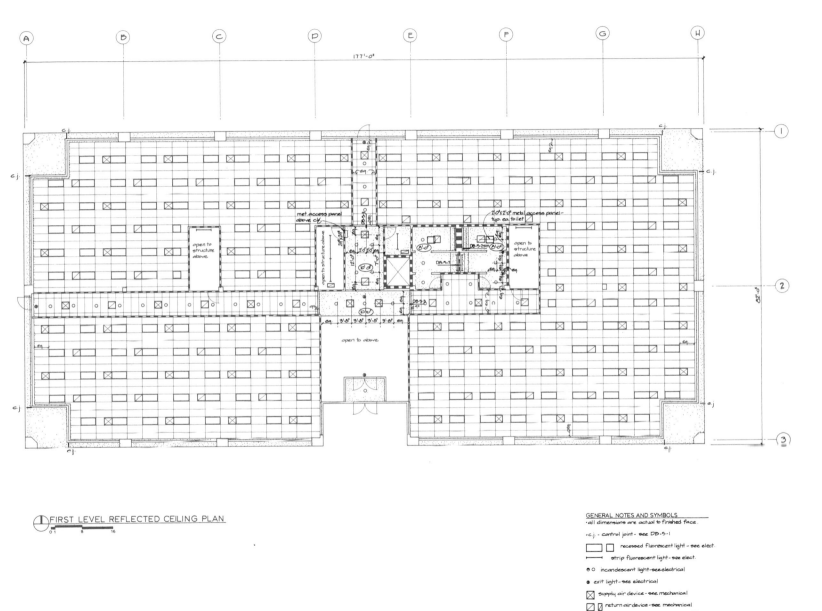

A
B
C
D
E
F
G
H

177'-0"

1
2
3

c.j.
c.j.
c.j.
c.j.
c.j.
c.j.
c.j.

open to
structure
above

open to
structure
above

open to
structure
above

open to above

met access panel
above c.v.

2'-0"x2'-0" metal access panel -
typ. ea. toilet

eq 3'-0" 3'-0" 3'-0" 3'-0" eq

① FIRST LEVEL REFLECTED CEILING PLAN

0 1   8   16

A
SPECULATIVE
OFFICE
BUILDING

in
DUGONE COUNTY
for

NICHOLAS
PROPERTIES

GENW, PC
architect

BUILDINGS R US
engineers

ISSUE

DATE:

FIRST LEVEL
REFLECTED
CEILING PLAN

A-5

■ **The Completed First Level Reflected Ceiling Plan**

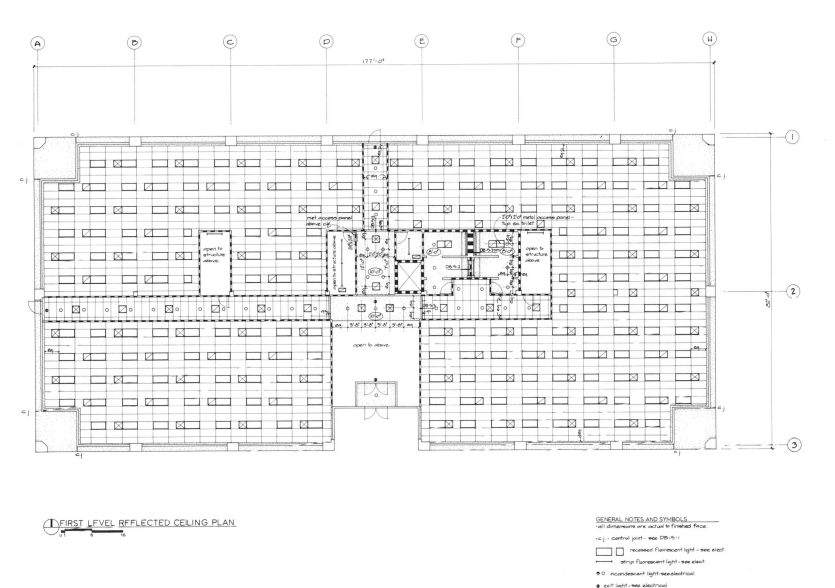

FIRST LEVEL REFLECTED CEILING PLAN

GENERAL NOTES AND SYMBOLS

· all dimensions are actual to finished face.

· c.j. - control joint - see DD-5-1

▭ ▯ recessed fluorescent light - see elect.

—— strip fluorescent light - see elect.

● ○ incandescent light - see electrical

◉ exit light - see electrical

⊠ supply air device - see mechanical

▨ return air device - see mechanical

· all ceiling heights 9'-0" unless noted ⬭

▬▬▬ partition penetrating ceiling plane

177'-0"

■ **Phase II**

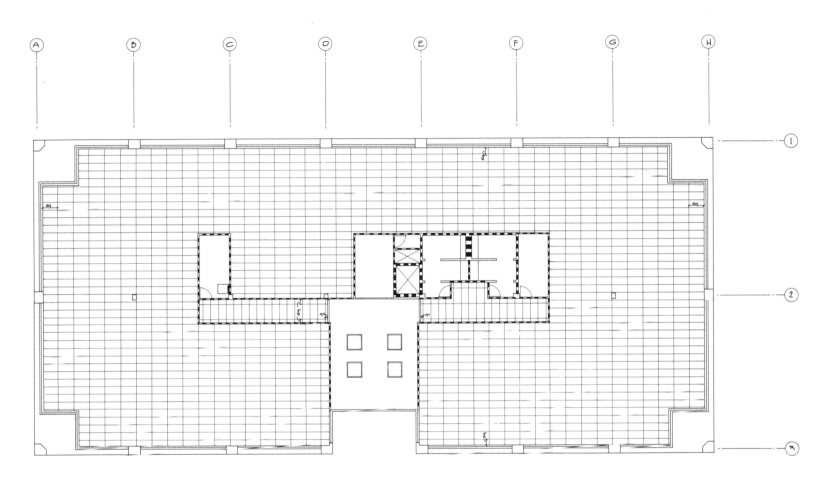

A B C D E F G H

1

2

3

SECOND LEVEL REFLECTED CEILING PLAN
0 1   8   16

A
SPECULATIVE
OFFICE
BUILDING
in
DUGONE COUNTY
for
NICHOLAS
PROPERTIES

GENW, PC.
architect

BUILDINGS R US
engineers

ISSUE:

DATE:

SECOND LEVEL
REFLECTED
CEILING PLAN

A-6

■ **Phase III**

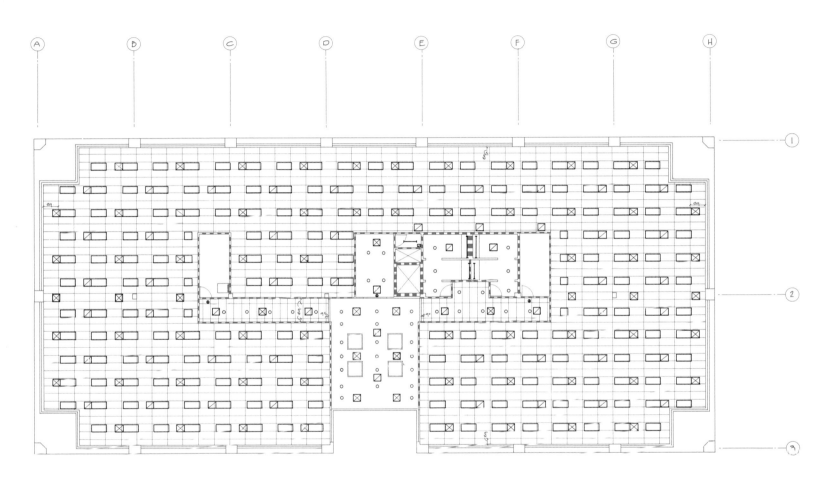

A
B
C
D
E
F
G
H

1

2

3

1 SECOND LEVEL REFLECTED CEILING PLAN
0 1   8   16

A
SPECULATIVE
OFFICE
BUILDING
in
DUGONE COUNTY
for

NICHOLAS
PROPERTIES

GENW, PC
architect

BUILDINGS R US
engineers

ISSUE

DATE:

SECOND LEVEL
REFLECTED
CEILING PLAN

A-6

■ **Phase IV**

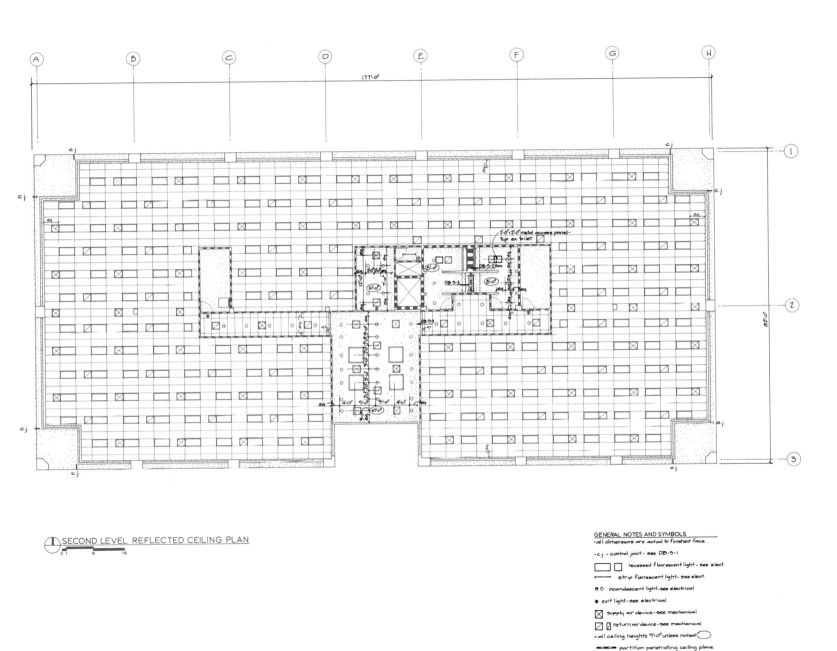

A
SPECULATIVE
OFFICE
BUILDING
in
DUGONE COUNTY
for

NICHOLAS
PROPERTIES

GEN W, PC
architect
BUILDINGS R US
engineers

ISSUE:

DATE:

SECOND LEVEL
REFLECTED
CEILING PLAN

A-6

177'-0"

82'-0"

2'-0" x 2'-0" metal access panel-
typ. ea. toilet

SECOND LEVEL REFLECTED CEILING PLAN

0 1   8   16

GENERAL NOTES AND SYMBOLS
· all dimensions are actual to finished face.

· c.j. - control joint - see DB-5-1

▭ ▯ recessed fluorescent light - see elect.

— strip fluorescent light - see elect.

⊙ ○ incandescent light - see electrical

● exit light - see electrical

☒ supply air device - see mechanical

▨ return air device - see mechanical

· all ceiling heights 9'-0" unless noted ◯

▬▬ partition penetrating ceiling plane

■ The Completed Second Level Reflected Ceiling Plan

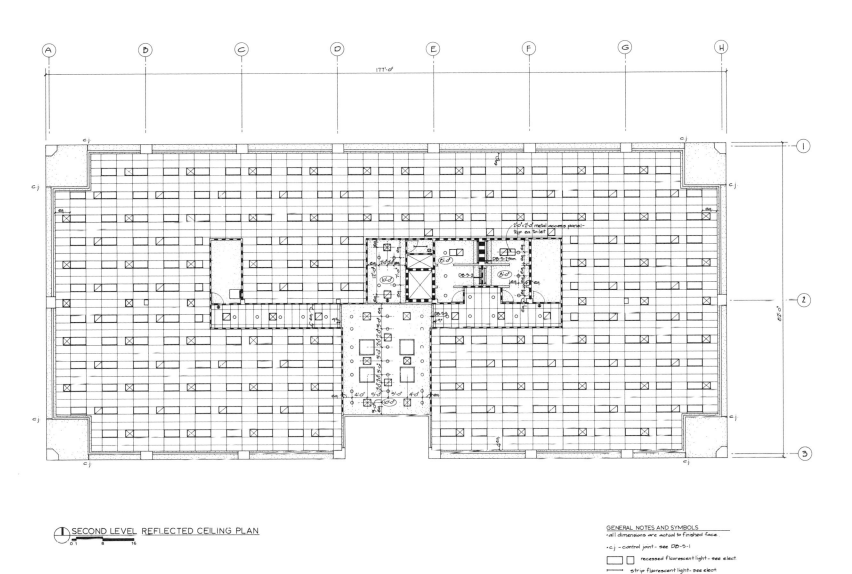

A B C D E F G H

177'-0"

82'-0"

1
2
3

c.j.

① SECOND LEVEL REFLECTED CEILING PLAN
0 1   8   16

2'-0"x 2'-0" metal access panel -
typ. ea. toilet
DB-5-2.5in.
DB-5-2

A
SPECULATIVE
OFFICE
BUILDING
in
DUGONE COUNTY
for
NICHOLAS
PROPERTIES

GEN W, PC.
architect
BUILDINGS R US
engineers

ISSUE:

DATE:

SECOND LEVEL
REFLECTED
CEILING PLAN

A-6

6 Exterior Elevations

Exterior elevations, like floor plans, contain a great number of cross-references to other drawings in the set of construction documents. They also show information that is important for the engineering consultants to be aware of when doing their work. Because of this need to provide reference information, exterior elevations are usually started along with the floor plans as the first documents produced in the set.

■ General Information

The mechanical consultant will be especially interested in building materials and their locations with regard to orientation, the extent of glazing, locations of overhangs and/or window setbacks, and acceptable (in terms of architectural design) locations for features such as fire department connections, inspector's test areas, hose bibs, and so forth.

The electrical consultant will be interested in the locations of exterior building lighting that will be building-mounted, while the structural consultant will want to know about the elevations of major features and the general configuration of the building's skin.

In drawing exterior elevations, you need to picture what a particular face of a building is going to look like when it is built. The ground line at the building should be drafted as a heavy line, which indicates the finished grades at the building's face. As the purpose of the exterior elevations are to show only the building, no landscaping should be added to the drawing. You should also avoid the use of shade and shadow on the drawings.

Exterior elevations should be drafted at a scale that will provide an adequate and clear presentation of all of the information that is required for the drawing. It is good practice to draft exterior elevations at the same scale as the floor plan. By using the same scale, you will give the set of construction documents a degree of consistency that will make them easier to use. Using the same scale also tends to speed up the process of drafting, as a certain amount of the elevation's configuration can be traced off of the floor plan.

When locating the exterior elevations on the document sheet, you should follow the general strategy for sheet composition that has been described in Chapter 1 by locating the first drawing in the upper-right-hand corner of the sheet. In many cases, however, only one or two elevations will actually fit onto a sheet. In these instances it is best to locate the elevation toward the right-hand side of the sheet, away from the binding edge. On the vertical axis of the sheet, you should attempt to distribute the drawings in such a manner that the composition is balanced.

Because few buildings will be perfect rectangles that have no steps in their façades, the question will often arise as to whether or not all of the "nooks" of the building need to be elevated. For example, on the south elevation of the building shown in this book, the entrance has been set back several feet from the face of the main building. In drafting the south elevation, you will not see the "nooks" facing east and west that lead back to the entrance. The guideline used in this book for drafting these elevations deals primarily with their construction and appearance as it relates to adjacent walls. If the construction technique does not vary from the adjacent wall, there will be no need to draft the "nook" elevation. Rather, it will be appropriate to note it as "similar" to the adjacent wall. The window frame type, if present, should also be noted, along with any other hidden features that might need to be mentioned. If the hidden elevation is not drafted, this noting is essential.

If, however, there is a change of construction or surface appearance, or if the elevation can not be clearly referenced to an adjacent wall, the hidden elevation should be drafted. In terms of drawing sequence, these hidden elevations should be shown immediately after the main elevation.

A similar question is whether two elevations that are virtually identical to each other will both need to be shown. As a rule, when two elevations are identical or almost identical to each other, there is no need to show them both. For example, in the illustrations shown on pages 92–99, exterior elevations on the west and on the east are almost identical. The only real difference in the two is that a door has been located on the ground level of one elevation and not on the other. In such a case you have three choices: to draft both elevations; to draft one elevation and note the other as "similar," and add a list of notes describing their differences; or to draft a partial elevation of the different condition and note that the parts that have not been shown are similar to the primary elevation. Any of these methods would be an acceptable approach to the situation. However, if all things are equal, you should always choose the fastest method. For this reason the example in this book shows only the east elevation and notes the differences that would be present in the west elevation.

Exterior elevations should have virtually no dimensions drafted on them. Occasionally the height of an exterior feature such as a light or a mechanical device will need to be located in elevation. These, however, should be located by an elevation bullet and not by a dimension string. The bullet should make reference to either the height that the object is above the finished floor or the height that the object is relative to grade. If dimensions are unavoidable, the "actual" system of dimensioning, which has been described in Chapter 3, is the the most appropriate choice.

The reason that dimensions are left off of exterior elevations as much as possible is to avoid redundancy. Virtually all of the features of exterior elevations that could be dimensioned on these drawings will be more clearly dimensioned in other locations within the set of construction documents.

Finally, in developing a strategy for showing material indications on the exterior elevations, you should make several considerations. It is very important for these elevations to have material indications shown, as the addition of this graphic information helps to clarify exactly what the building is supposed to look like. Frequently, however, you will find that large expanses of a building have the same materials, and that material indications will be repetitive and time-consuming to draft. In these cases, it is acceptable to draft a two- to three-inch-wide diagonal strip of the material indications with appropriate noting. To get a better sense of this method of drafting material indications, refer to the example shown on pages 98–99.

■ Appropriate Notes and Symbols

Finished floor elevations should be clearly labeled with a bullet that has been drafted on the right-hand side of the elevation, about one inch back from the actual drawing. Miscellaneous features that require elevation notation should also be labeled with a bullet that is located adjacent to the feature being referenced.

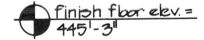

finish floor elev. = 445'-3"

Dimensions, when necessary, should be in short strings that are continuous when possible. Where a dimension intersects a column centerline, the intersection should be marked with a dot. Where a dimension string intersects any other feature, that intersection should be marked with a slash drawn at a 45-degree angle. The slash should slope from left to right for vertical dimensions and from right to left for horizontal dimensions.

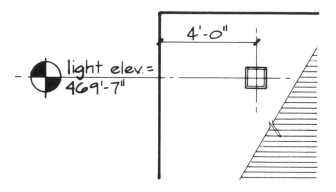

Column centerlines and column designation bubbles should be drafted in such a way that the centerline does not run through the entire elevation, but rather stops about ½" away from the edge of the drawing. The size of the centerline bubble should be appropriate for the designation to be labeled within it. All bubbles should be the same size and should be located at the top of the elevation. Bubbles should also be drafted several inches away from the drawing of the exterior elevation.

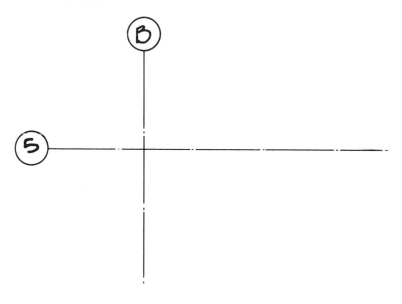

Cross-referencing cuts—wall sections. The arrow symbol shown refers to a wall section that is located on another sheet within the set of construction documents. Underneath the arrow is a number to help locate the section. The first number refers to the sheet number, while the second number refers to the particular drawing on the sheet. The size of the arrowhead is not critical, although once a size has been selected, it should be held constant. A good system for drawing arrows is to make the bottom of the arrow a minimum of ⅜" and to draw the sides with the 30-degree side of a 30/60 triangle.

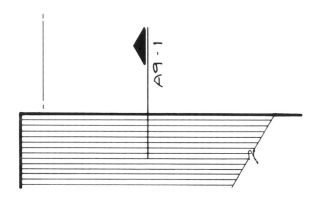

Cross-referencing cuts—building section. This next symbol refers to a building section that has been located on another sheet within the set of construction documents. The bottom number refers to the sheet number, while the top number refers to the particular drawing on the sheet. The size of the circle should be such that it can easily contain the information that is labeled inside of it. Once a size is selected, all circles should be consistent and adhere to the standard.

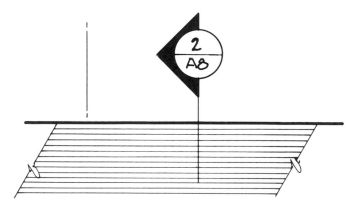

A control joint in exterior finish materials should be drafted as a thin double line with the note "CJ" located next to it. Frequently control joints will occur along known features such as column centerlines. In these instances, where locations are graphically clear, no dimensioning is required. If, however, the control joint does not occur in an obvious location, it should be dimensioned with reference to a known feature to ensure that it will not be located in a haphazard fashion. You should refer to the construction standards of the particular industry whose materials are used on the exterior elevations for their recommendations about appropriate spacings and locations for control joints.

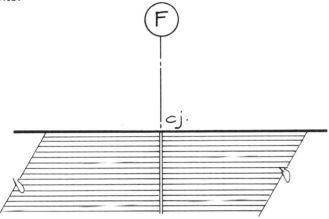

Window frame types should be indicated with a reference number placed within a polygon that is on the window that is being referenced. The size of the polygon is not critical, but should be held consistent for the entire set of documents. Every window that is unique should receive a number. Identical windows may share a number. Keep in mind, however, that identical, in this case, means that the head, sill, and jambs are also identical. The window frame type refers to an enlarged elevation of the window and frame that has been shown elsewhere in the document set. All of the details for the window will be referenced from the enlarged elevation.

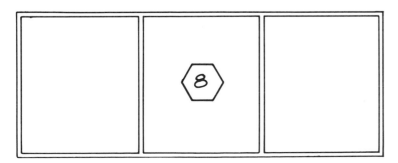

Other features that should be drafted on the exterior elevations might include special graphics, signs, roof scuppers, and graphic representations of special finish detailing (such as rowlocks or soldier courses in brick). All details should be referenced to the detail book by either an arrow cut or reference circle with a reference number.

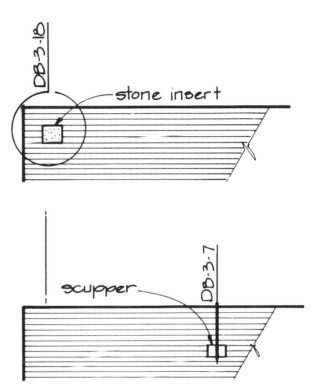

All material indications should be drawn in accordance with the standards that are described in Chapter 1.

■ **Sequence of the Documentation Procedure**
The exterior elevations are drafted in three phases. This drawing is completed ahead of most of the other drawings in the document set and thus does not have a fourth phase.

■ Phase I

The initial work to be performed for the exterior elevations is to draft all of the façades of the building. As with the drawing of the floor plans, this requires a tremendous amount of work. It is important to get as much information as possible shown on the sheet so that you can begin detailed conversations with the engineering consultants.

The Phase I drawing contains the bulk of the information that will be shown on the exterior elevation construction documents. You must first draft the building mass and all fenestration. Column centerlines and bubble designations are also drafted at this stage, along with all finished floor elevations.

From a sequencing perspective, it is best to first draft the column centerlines and finish floor bullets. These two references will become the core around which the rest of the elevation can be drafted.

The drawings on the sheet are next given their titles, scales, and reference numbers. The information in the title block should also be filled in properly at this time.

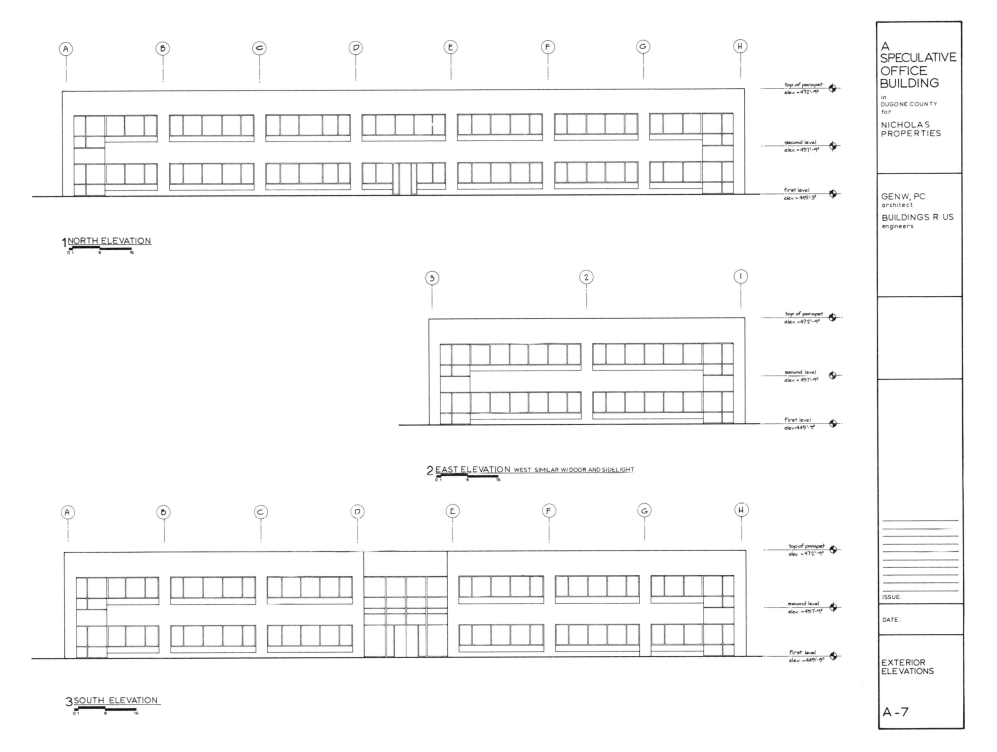

1 NORTH ELEVATION

2 EAST ELEVATION WEST SIMILAR W/ DOOR AND SIDELIGHT

3 SOUTH ELEVATION

top of parapet
elev. = 472'-9"

second level
elev. = 457'-9"

first level
elev. = 445'-3"

A
SPECULATIVE
OFFICE
BUILDING
in
DUGONE COUNTY
for
NICHOLAS
PROPERTIES

GENW, PC
architect

BUILDINGS R US
engineers

ISSUE:

DATE:

EXTERIOR
ELEVATIONS

A-7

■ Phase II

In the second phase of the exterior elevation documentation you should add cross-referencing. Locations of building sections and wall sections are indicated and referenced. Almost all of the notes for the drawing are also now added to the sheet, including references to the window frame types and control joints.

Note that structural foundations are also drafted in this phase. This information should be available from the structural consultant at this point in the project or from estimates that you can prepare based on guideline information available from the appropriate trades. Be sure to use broken lines to indicate foundations as they are below grade and not visible.

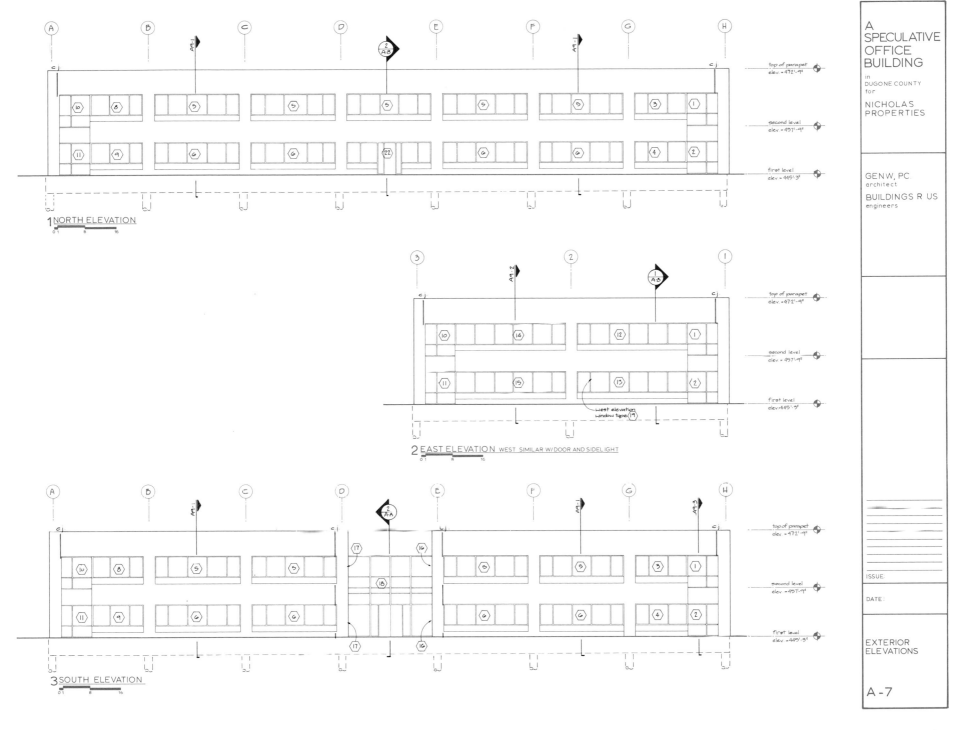

1 NORTH ELEVATION

2 EAST ELEVATION WEST SIMILAR W/DOOR AND SIDELIGHT

3 SOUTH ELEVATION

west elevation
window type (19)

top of parapet
elev. = 472'-9"

second level
elev. = 457'-9"

first level
elev. = 445'-3"

A
SPECULATIVE
OFFICE
BUILDING
in
DUGONE COUNTY
for
NICHOLAS
PROPERTIES

GEN W, PC
architect

BUILDINGS R US
engineers

ISSUE:

DATE:

EXTERIOR
ELEVATIONS

A-7

■ Phase III

In the third phase of the exterior elevation documentation you should add material indications. As mentioned previously, material indications are of particular importance for the exterior elevations and they should always be added to the final document. The material indications on the example drawing have been drafted in the strip method that was described on page 89.

Phase III, which is the final phase for exterior elevations documentation, is also the appropriate time to add any miscellaneous notes that might be needed to adequately describe all of the important features of the drawing. Although there will typically be little that would be noted in this manner on the elevations, it is critical that all features of the building be described, even if they are not detailed. This will ensure their inclusion in the final building.

You should also check the drawing at this time. All cross-referencing and notes should be verified, along with all elevations that have been indicated with a bullet.

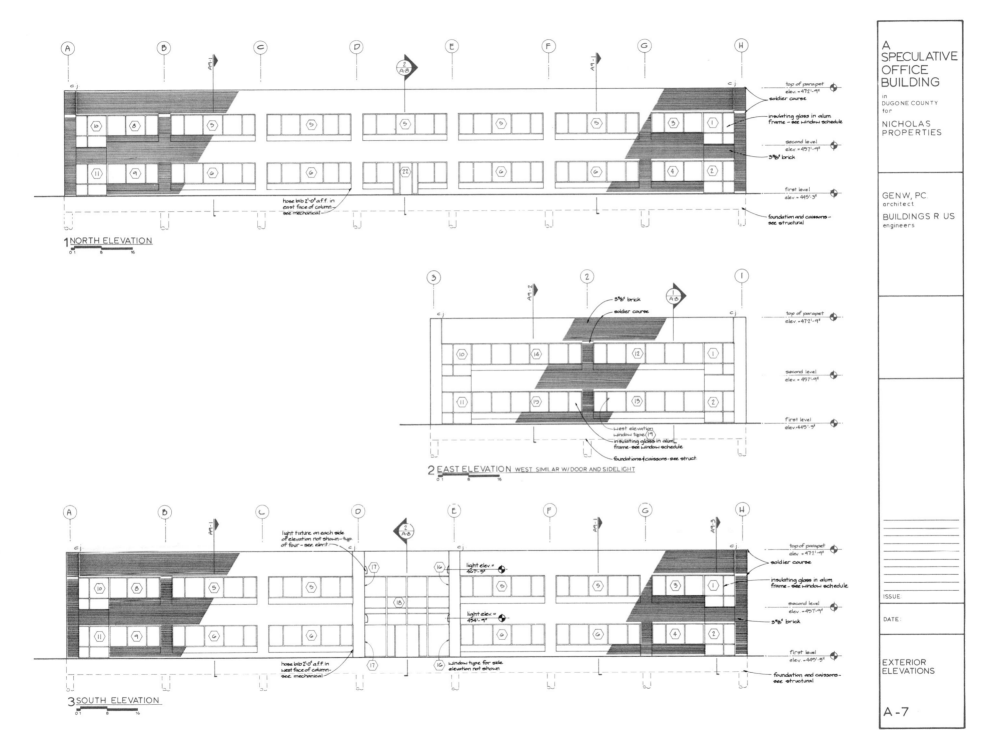

1 NORTH ELEVATION
0 1   8   16

2 EAST ELEVATION WEST SIMILAR W/ DOOR AND SIDELIGHT
0 1   8   16

3 SOUTH ELEVATION
0 1   8   16

A
SPECULATIVE
OFFICE
BUILDING

in
DUGONE COUNTY
for

NICHOLAS
PROPERTIES

GEN W, PC.
architect

BUILDINGS R US
engineers

ISSUE:

DATE:

EXTERIOR
ELEVATIONS

A-7

■ **The Completed Exterior Elevations**

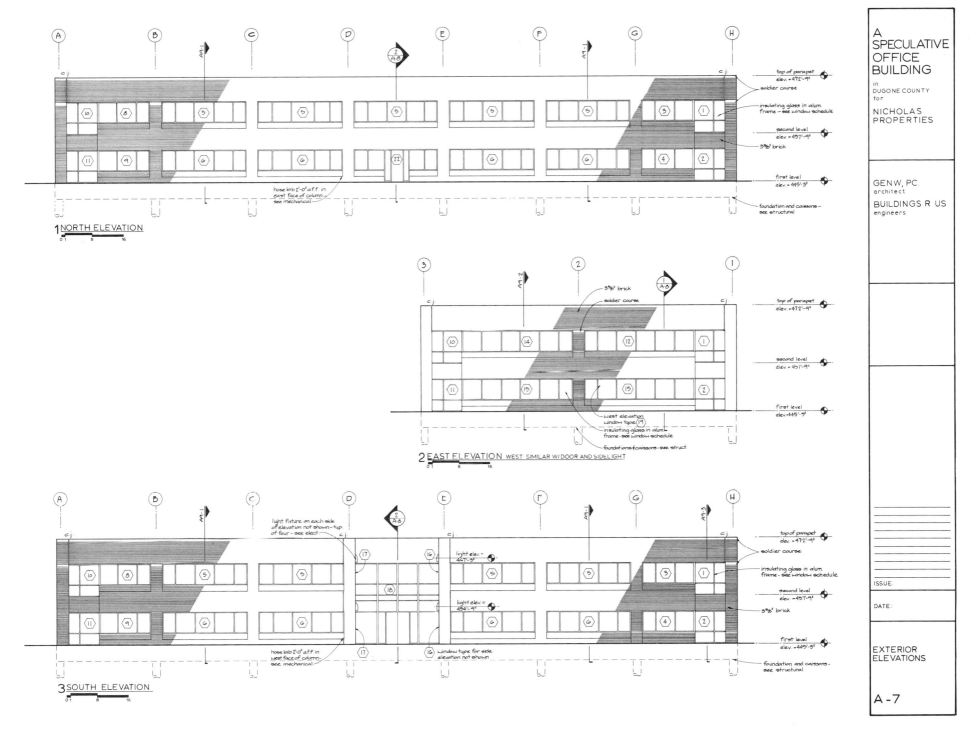

7 Building Sections

Building sections show how the general systems of a building fit together and relate to each other. The primary intent of these drawings is to convey architectural and structural relationships. It is common, however, to add mechanical and electrical references to the drawings. Because so much information is required from the consultants to adequately draw the building sections, you will not usually start on them until one-third to one-half of the way through the entire process of construction documentation. Building sections are rarely critical to the progress of other drawings, so this starting time is also consistent with staging of the production of the work.

■ General Information

Because building sections are intended to show general systems, you should be careful to avoid going into too much detail when doing the drafting. (This is not to say that there is never a reason to go into detail on the drawing.) In some cases, particularly on smaller projects, you may be able to show the entire building section at a large-enough scale so that separate wall section drawings are not needed. In these instances, detail would be required and information contained in Chapter 8, "Wall Sections," should be incorporated.

Building sections are drawn as if you are looking at a slice of the building that has been exposed by cutting the building into two sections with a knife. You see not only the architectural features of spaces, but also the structure of the building. All items should be shown in scale and in their correct locations, with particular care taken to show the correct slope of the roof. It is good practice to draft items that have been cut in section somewhat darker than items that are being seen in the background. It is also standard practice to omit material indications for these background items.

Building sections should be shown at the same scale as the exterior elevations. This will help to provide increased consistency in the construction document set. It may also save you some time, as there will be certain features that can be easily referenced or traced.

The number of building sections that should be shown for a given project is largely a matter of personal taste. Some architects do not even include building sections as a part of their construction documents. Others include a building section for any part of the structure that is unique. My own preference falls somewhere between these two options. I will typically show one transverse section and one longitudinal section for each extension of the building. The example in this book includes two building sections; in a Y-shaped building three or four building sections would be shown. When deciding where to cut the sections, you should select locations where the section will help to clarify the intent of the design and documents. Cutting a section in a particular location only because it will make the drafting easier is a poor approach; it would be better to draw nothing in the way of building sections than to pick unimportant locations that convey little if any important information.

Building sections, like exterior elevations, should have virtually no dimensions drafted on them. On the rare occasion that a feature needs to be dimensioned on the sections, the dimensioning should be done in short, continuous strings. It is best to use the "actual" system described in Chapter 3, which is consistent with the sequence of construction and the general stage of progress that the building will be at when this construction takes place. As with the exterior elevations, the primary reason for avoiding dimensions on the building sections is to avoid as much redundancy as possible in the production of the set of construction documents.

Material indications should be added to building sections whenever possible. Because these indications are only drafted for areas that are cut by the section, they are relatively quick and easy to draft. Materials that would require more time to draft, such as earth, can be bled in the manner shown in the sample building sections on pages 108–9.

■ Appropriate Notes and Symbols
Finished floor elevations should be clearly labeled with a bullet. This bullet should be drafted on the right-hand side of the building section, around one inch away from the actual drawing.

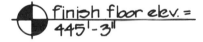

Dimensions, when necessary, should be in short strings that are continuous when possible. When a dimension string intersects a column centerline, the intersection should be marked with a dot. When a dimension string intersects any other feature, that intersection should be marked with a slash drawn at a 45-degree angle. The slash should angle from left to right for vertical dimensions and from right to left for horizontal dimensions.

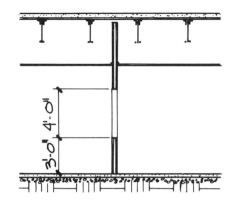

Column centerlines and column designation bubbles should be drafted in such a way that the centerline runs through the entire building section, including the structural foundations, footings, and caissons. The size of the centerline bubble should be appropriate for the designation to be labeled within it. All bubbles should be the same size and should be located at the top of and several inches away from the building section.

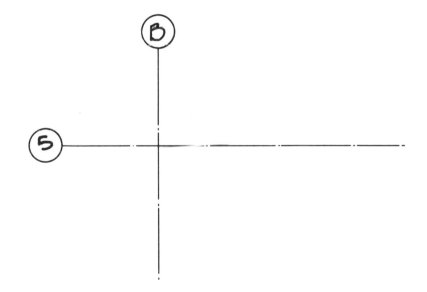

Structural features such as caissons, footings, and foundation walls should be drafted. These features should be shown with solid lines when they are actually cut, and with broken lines when they are beyond the area that has been cut.

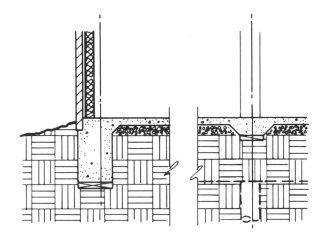

Cross-referencing cuts—building sections. The cross-reference cut symbol shown below refers to other building sections that have been located on the same sheet or on a different sheet within the set of construction documents. The bottom number refers to the sheet number and the top number to the particular drawing on that sheet. The size of the circle should be such that it can easily contain the information that is labeled inside of it. Once a size is selected, all circles should adhere to that standard.

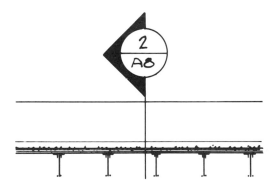

Room names and numbers should be taken from the floor plan and drafted in lettering that is slightly larger and bolder than the standard. If a room name and number will not fit into the room itself, they should be located close to the room with a leader referencing them appropriately.

(standard) men
141

Because the building sections can be cut at any condition in the building, there are many features that might be appropriate for inclusion on the drawing. The guideline is simple: If the section cuts through a feature, that feature should be shown. If a feature is beyond the section cut, it should be shown only if it is significant. In an effort to avoid redundancy, details should only be referenced on building sections when they cannot be referenced in any other location in the set of construction documents. When details are cut, they should be referenced to the detail book by either a cut arrow with a reference number or by a reference circle with a reference number.

All material indications should be drawn in accordance with the standards that are described in Chapter 1.

■ Sequence of the Documentation Procedure

There are two phases in the preparation of building sections. Whether you should start the document at Phase II or Phase III will depend on how quickly you have been able to design the roof slopes, obtain sufficient information from the structural consultant to correctly draft the structure, and get ductwork sizes from the mechanical consultant. There is no need to draft the section when you are lacking the information to do so properly. The examples in this book assume that Phases I and II were not used in the preparation of the building sections.

Phase I
Not used.

Phase II
Not used.

■ Phase III

Because this document is started late in the construction documentation process, there will be sufficient information from the engineering consultants to assure the architect that the time spent drafting will not be wasted. Also, since building sections are rather easy to draft quickly, it is safe to assume that a great deal of information will be able to be drafted during this initial phase.

The drawing at the right shows one transverse and one longitudinal section. By drafting the column centerlines first and then adding in the finished floor elevations, you will find it is a simple matter to draft in the building. In certain areas some time can be saved by tracing the locations of elements, such as interior partitions, from the floor plans.

Although nothing is labeled at this phase, all of the drafting for the building sections is performed. Wall sections, which were started during Phase II, are indicated in less detail on the building sections. Roof slopes are shown to match the drainage design, which was also determined during the second phase of construction documentation. Thicknesses and types of structure are shown based on information that you have received from the structural consultant or determined from guideline information from the appropriate trades. Architectural features are shown to the extent that they are known. Thus, at the end of this phase, the building sections are essentially complete in terms of graphic information.

The last items that you add to the sheet in this phase are the titles, scales, and all title block information.

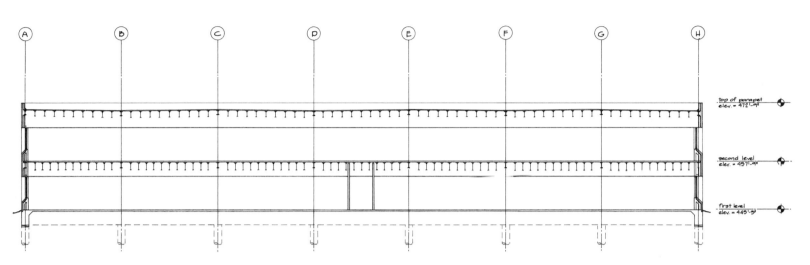

Ⓐ Ⓑ Ⓒ Ⓓ Ⓔ Ⓕ Ⓖ Ⓗ

top of parapet
elev. = 472'-9"

second level
elev. = 457'-4"

first level
elev. = 445'-3"

1 LONGITUDINAL SECTION

0 1   8   16

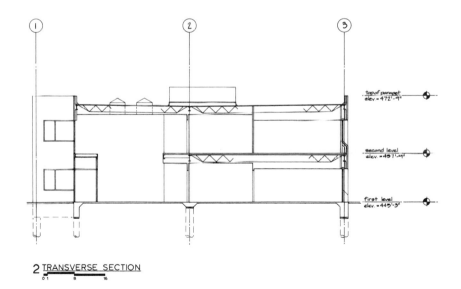

① ② ③

top of parapet
elev. = 472'-9"

second level
elev. = 457'-4"

first level
elev. = 445'-3"

2 TRANSVERSE SECTION

0 1   8   16

A
SPECULATIVE
OFFICE
BUILDING

in
DUGONE COUNTY
for

NICHOLAS
PROPERTIES

GENW, PC.
architect

BUILDINGS R US
engineers

ISSUE:

DATE:

BUILDING
SECTIONS

A-8

■ Phase IV

This phase, which is the last phase in the documentation of the building sections, is when you add the notes and other miscellaneous items of reference that are needed for the document. Material indications are also drafted.

The drawings are also checked and any notes that are necessary to describe features that might not have been detailed are added.

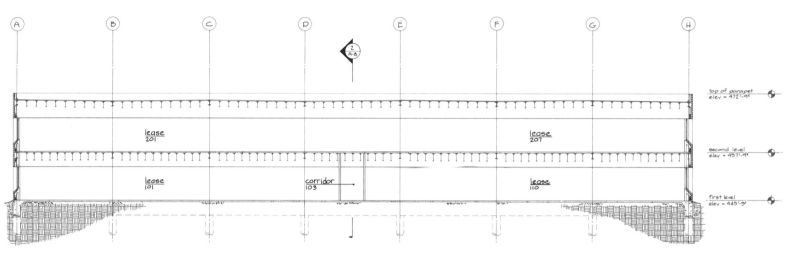

A B C D E F G H

2 / A-8

top of parapet
elev.= 472'-9"

lease
201

lease
207

second level
elev.= 457'-9"

lease
101

corridor
103

lease
110

first level
elev.= 445'-3"

1 LONGITUDINAL SECTION
0 1   8   16

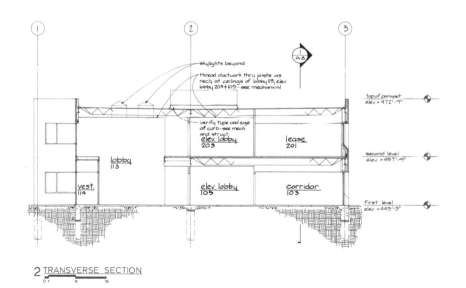

1 2 3

1 / A-8

skylights beyond

thread ductwork thru joists as
necy at ceilings of lobby 113, elev.
lobby 203 & 105 - see mechanical

top of parapet
elev.= 472'-9"

verify type and size
of curb - see mech.
and struct.

elev. lobby
203

lease
201

second level
elev.= 457'-9"

lobby
113

elev. lobby
105

corridor
103

vest.
114

first level
elev.= 445'-3"

2 TRANSVERSE SECTION
0 1   8   16

A
SPECULATIVE
OFFICE
BUILDING
in
DUGONE COUNTY
for
NICHOLAS
PROPERTIES

GENW, PC
architect
BUILDINGS R US
engineers

ISSUE:

DATE:

BUILDING
SECTIONS

A-8

■ The Completed Building Sections

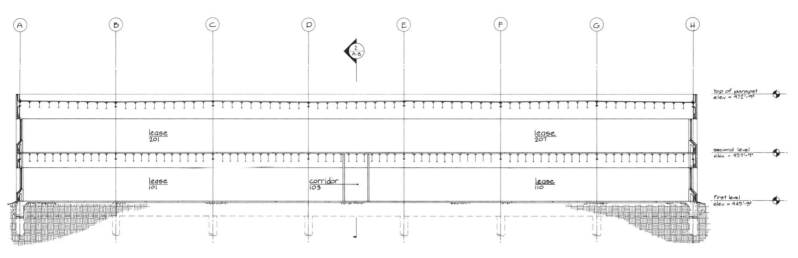

A B C D E F G H

2 / A-8

lease
201

lease
207

top of parapet
elev. = 472'-9"

second level
elev. = 457'-9"

lease
101

corridor
103

lease
110

first level
elev. = 445'-3"

1 LONGITUDINAL SECTION

0 1   8   16

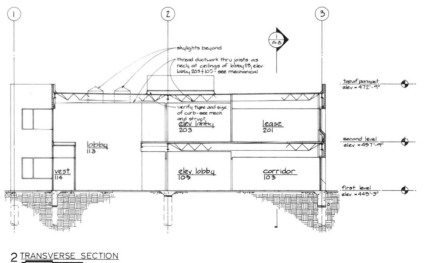

1   2   3

1 / A-8

skylights beyond

thread ductwork thru joists as
nec'y at ceilings of lobby 113, elev.
bbby 203 + 103 - see mechanical

top of parapet
elev. = 472'-9"

verify type and size
of curb - see mech.
and struct.

elev. lobby
203

lease
201

second level
elev. = 457'-9"

lobby
113

vest.
114

elev. lobby
103

corridor
103

first level
elev. = 445'-3"

2 TRANSVERSE SECTION

0 1   8   16

A
SPECULATIVE
OFFICE
BUILDING
IN
DUGONE COUNTY
for
NICHOLAS
PROPERTIES

GENW, PC.
architect
BUILDINGS R US
engineers

ISSUE

DATE :

BUILDING
SECTIONS

A-8

8 Wall Sections

For many designers there is no fate worse than having to figure out and then draft the wall sections. Drafting wall sections requires a more complete knowledge of building assembly than any other major construction document. Only certain details, which are included in the detail book, require a more extensive knowledge of assemblies. It is easy to see why architects often tend to procrastinate the drafting of wall sections. It is important, however, to get an early start on these drawings.

■ General Information

The construction of exterior walls will vary from project to project, with typical conditions being rare. Each exterior building material will have its own set of requirements for wall construction. Thus, there is little that can be said about the assembly of exterior walls that is of a sufficiently general nature that you could be comfortable applying it to every situation. Essentially all that can be categorized is that there will usually be at least three areas comprising the thickness of an exterior wall: the exterior finish material, an air space, and the framing system that is being used to support the interior finishes and/or the exterior finish. Obviously the construction of a brick wall will be quite different from the construction of an all-glass curtain wall system. You should consult the manufacturers' literature for guidance on the proper means of construction for the exterior-finish system that you select.

Although the construction of the actual wall will vary substantially from project to project, the approach to the preparation of the wall sections for construction documents will be consistent. Wall sections are shown as if the given wall had been sliced open with a knife to reveal its contents. You see, in detail, the relationship between finish materials and structural materials. As with building sections, material indications should only be drafted for areas that are being cut. Features that are shown beyond should be indicated by showing their outlines in light linework.

Wall sections should be shown at a scale that is appropriate for conveying the level of information that they must provide. Typical scales include ½" = 1'-0", ¾" = 1'-0", and 1" = 1'-0". You should also consider the height of the wall section. The drawing should show the entire section from the bottom of its structure to the top of its parapet. In taller buildings, however, this may not be possible because of the vertical height of the wall section. When this occurs, it is most typical to do cuts on the wall section, whereby large areas of the wall that have the same construction are only partially drafted. Where similar parts are not shown, cut lines are drafted indicating that a section of the drawing has not been executed. By using these cuts you can compress the wall section into a series of small drawings, thereby enabling a very large section to fit into a smaller drawing area.

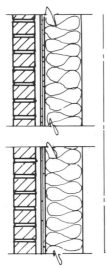

When locating wall sections on the sheet, you should follow the standards described in Chapter 1, locating the first section (which should be the most typical) on the right-hand side of the sheet. Moving toward the left-hand side of the sheet, draft the subsequent sections. Take care to leave ample room for notes, as wall sections require a great deal of space for their written descriptions.

People frequently question how many wall sections should be shown, and where they should be cut on the building. The answers are simple. Any condition at a building's exterior wall that is different from any other condition must be shown. This matter of different conditions includes structural features as well as architectural features. If, for example, you have two exterior walls that are identically constructed except for the direction in which the structural joists are running, you will have to draft them both. Some architects do not draft each condition, choosing to label one of the sections as a "similar" condition or to draft only a partial wall section of the different condition to save time in the construction documents process. However, wall sections often reveal problems in the proposed building assembly that have been overlooked; the exercise of exploring all of the different conditions helps to make a more sound project.

■ Appropriate Notes and Symbols

Finished floor elevations should be clearly labeled with a bullet that has been drafted on the right-hand side of the wall section, around ½" away from the actual drawing. Miscellaneous features that require elevation notation should also be labeled with a bullet that is located adjacent to the feature being referenced.

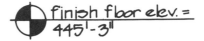

Dimensions should be in generally continuous strings. Short strings should be avoided. When a dimension string intersects a column centerline, the intersection should be marked with a dot. When a dimension string intersects any other feature, that intersection should be marked with a slash drawn at a 45-degree angle, sloping from left to right for the vertical dimension and from right to left for the horizontal dimension.

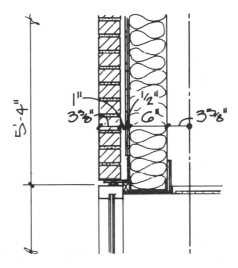

Column centerlines and column designation bubbles should be drafted in such a way that the centerline runs through the entire wall section. Drawn as a series of long lines with single dashes, the column centerline is the basic reference point for all horizontal dimensions. The size of the centerline bubble should be appropriate for the designation to be labeled within it. All bubbles should be the same size and should be located at the top of the wall section. Bubbles should be held away from the actual drawing several inches to allow space for dimensions lines.

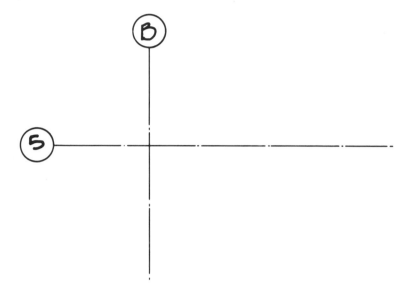

Structural features such as slabs, foundations, footings, and caissons should be shown. If these features are actually cut, they should be drafted as solid lines. If, however, they are in the distance, they should be drafted as broken lines.

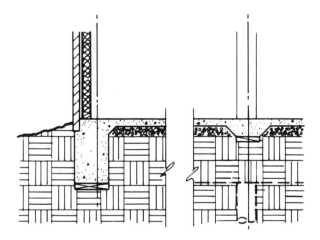

Wall sections will have many references to architectural details in the detail book that should be drafted at the same time as the wall section. These details can be referenced to the detail book by either a cut arrow with a reference number or by a reference circle with a reference number.

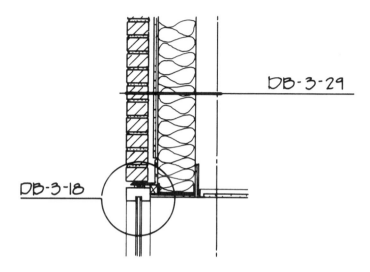

All material indications should be drawn in accordance with the standards that are described in Chapter 1.

■ Sequence of the Documentation Procedure

There are three phases in the preparation of wall sections. Because the first phase is not used, these descriptions start with Phase II.

Phase I

Not used.

■ Phase II

In the first phase of drafting the floor plans (see page 34), an assumption was made about the particular construction assembly for the exterior walls. The assembly that was selected consists of 3⅝" brick, a 1" air space, ½" sheathing, 6" structural steel studs, and ⅝" gypsum board. The decision was also made to situate the wall with a relationship to the structural column that would allow a small contingency for unforeseen revisions to the column sizing.

Thus, for this phase of the construction documentation of the wall sections, you know the construction of the wall assembly and the location of the column centerline in relation to the wall. From the exterior elevations, which have already been started, you know the locations of and the heights of the glass above the finished floor. At this stage of documentation, a further assumption will be made that the glass will be 1" insulating glass set in a 2" by 4" framing system. This system is very common in commercial construction.

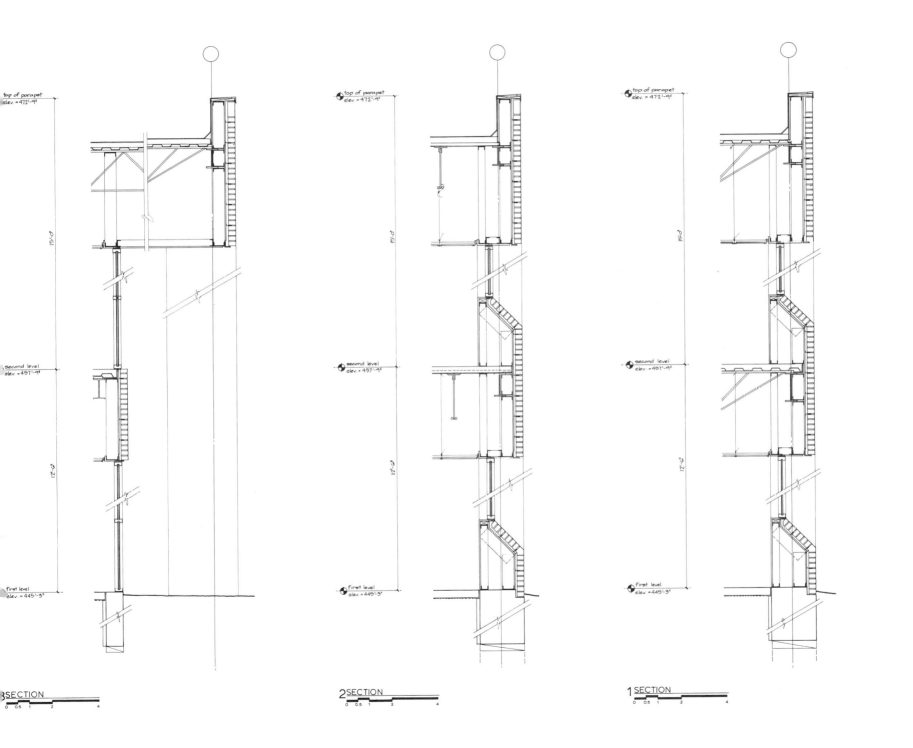

A
SPECULATIVE
OFFICE
BUILDING
in
DUGONE COUNTY
for

NICHOLAS
PROPERTIES

GENW, P.C.
architect

BUILDINGS R US
engineers

ISSUE:

DATE :

WALL SECTIONS

A-9

top of parapet
elev. = 472'-9"

15'-0"

second level
elev. = 457'-9"

12'-0"

first level
elev. = 445'-3"

3 SECTION
0 0.5 1   2   4

top of parapet
elev. = 472'-9"

15'-0"

second level
elev. = 457'-9"

12'-0"

first level
elev. = 445'-3"

2 SECTION
0 0.5 1   2   4

top of parapet
elev. = 472'-9"

15'-0"

second level
elev. = 457'-9"

12'-0"

first level
elev. = 445'-3"

1 SECTION
0 0.5 1   2   4

■ Phase III

In the third phase of the wall sections documentation features are added that were not available in the previous phase. In the example shown, a perimeter drainage system has been added.

The decision as to whether or not to use a perimeter drainage system will be dependent on recommendations from the soils consultant and the soils report. Expansive soils that are subject to moisture will almost always require a perimeter drain. It is important to provide a means of getting water that builds up away from the building's foundations and slabs.

"Slab on grade" refers to a concrete slab that is poured on grade but is not connected to the footings or caissons. This allows the slab to move up and down as the soil it rests on expands or contracts according to the moisture content of the soil. A structural slab, which is connected to the footings or caissons, will not move in this manner. Because they are so expensive, however, structural slabs are typically used only in areas where this movement is highly objectionable. In either case, a perimeter drainage system will help to reduce the movement stress by lowering the moisture content of the soil.

In this phase of the documentation you also add detail cross-referencing, more detailed dimensions, and notes. Notice that notes are typically arranged together into groups that describe particular assemblies. Also notice that only the first wall section is extensively noted. When similar conditions occur in the other wall sections, these conditions are referenced back to the first section. This practice saves time and avoids redundancy.

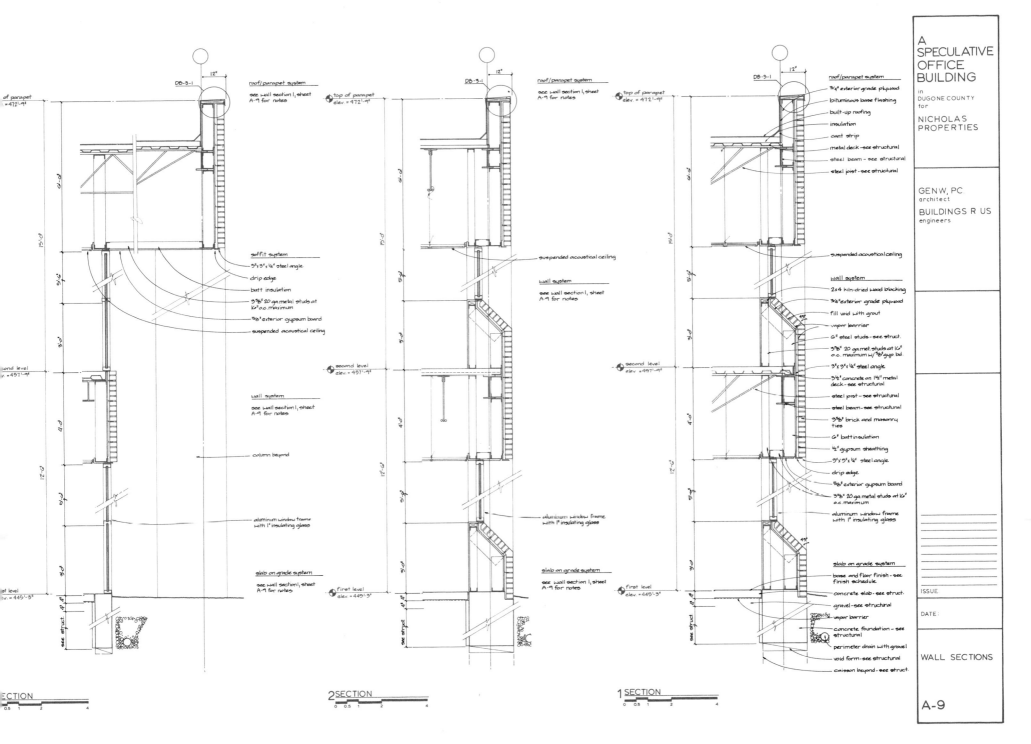

Left section (3):

roof/parapet system

see wall section 1, sheet A-9 for notes

of parapet = 472'-9"

soffit system
- 3"x3"x ¼" steel angle
- drip edge
- batt insulation
- 3⅝" 20 ga. metal studs at 16" o.c. maximum
- ⅝" exterior gypsum board
- suspended acoustical ceiling

wall system
see wall section 1, sheet A-9 for notes

column beyond

second level elev. = 457'-9"

slab on grade system
see wall section 1, sheet A-9 for notes

first level elev. = 445'-3"

aluminum window frame with 1" insulating glass

see struct.

15'-0"   12'-0"

Middle section (2):

DB-3-1   12"

top of parapet elev. = 472'-9"

roof/parapet system
see wall section 1, sheet A-9 for notes

suspended acoustical ceiling

wall system
see wall section 1, sheet A-9 for notes

second level elev. = 457'-9"

aluminum window frame with 1" insulating glass

slab on grade system
see wall section 1, sheet A-9 for notes

first level elev. = 445'-3"

15'-0"   12'-0"

2 SECTION
0 0.5 1   2   4

Right section (1):

DB-3-1   12"

top of parapet elev. = 472'-9"

roof/parapet system
- ¾" exterior grade plywood
- bituminous base flashing
- built-up roofing
- insulation
- cant strip
- metal deck - see structural
- steel beam - see structural
- steel post - see structural

suspended acoustical ceiling

wall system
- 2x4 kiln-dried wood blocking
- ¾" exterior grade plywood
- fill void with grout
- vapor barrier
- 6" steel studs - see struct.
- 3⅝" 20 ga. met. studs at 16" o.c. maximum w/ ⅝" gyp. bd.
- 3"x3"x ¼" steel angle
- 3½" concrete on 1½" metal deck - see structural
- steel post - see structural
- steel beam - see structural
- 3⅝" brick and masonry ties
- 6" batt insulation
- ½" gypsum sheathing
- 3"x3"x ¼" steel angle
- drip edge
- ⅝" exterior gypsum board
- 3⅝" 20 ga. metal studs at 16" o.c. maximum

second level elev. = 457'-9"

aluminum window frame with 1" insulating glass

slab on grade system
- base and floor finish - see finish schedule
- concrete slab - see struct.
- gravel - see structural
- vapor barrier
- concrete foundation - see structural
- perimeter drain with gravel
- void form - see structural
- caisson beyond - see struct.

first level elev. = 445'-9"

see struct.

15'-0"   12'-0"

1 SECTION
0 0.5 1   2   4

Far left:

SECTION
0.5 1   2   4

A
SPECULATIVE
OFFICE
BUILDING

in
DUGONE COUNTY
for

NICHOLAS
PROPERTIES

GEN W, PC
architect

BUILDINGS R US
engineers

ISSUE:

DATE:

WALL SECTIONS

A-9

■ Phase IV

In the final phase of the wall section documentation all material indications are added. These make the wall section clear graphically.

As always, all work should be checked at this stage of the documentation. All dimensions and detail references should be verified. Miscellaneous notes should be added to provide descriptions of items that might not have been detailed. Although this is always important for any construction document, it is especially critical for the wall sections. These drawings describe large areas of construction, and an oversight on them can be particularly troublesome.

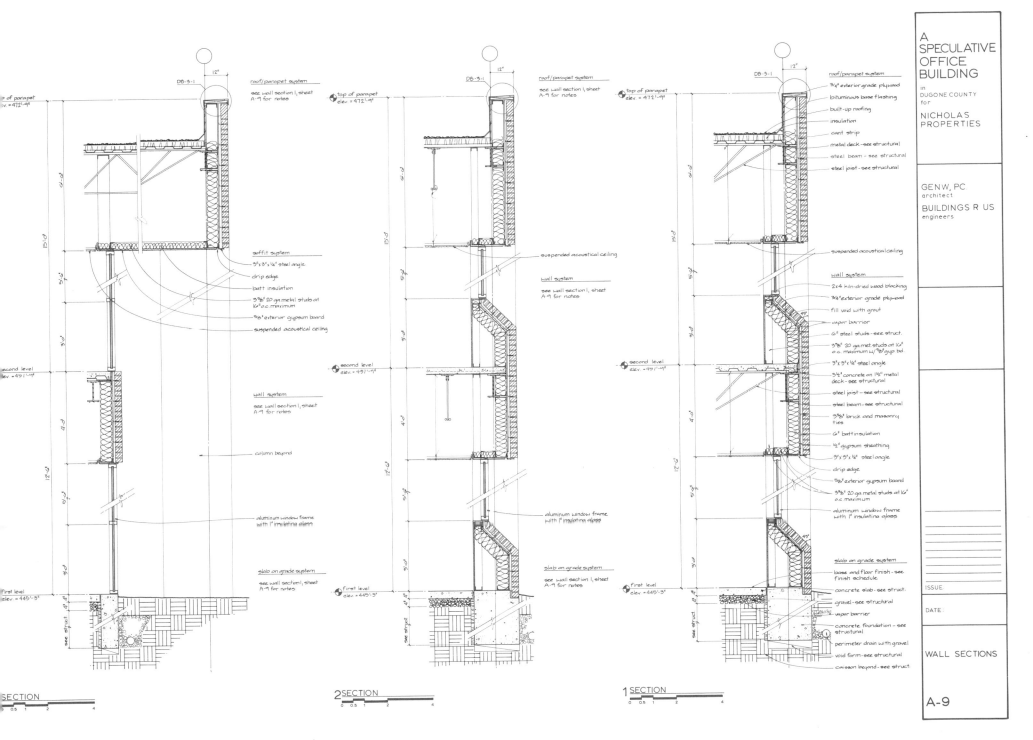

roof/parapet system
see wall section 1, sheet A-9 for notes

roof/parapet system
see wall section 1, sheet A-9 for notes

roof/parapet system
- ¾" exterior grade plywood
- bituminous base flashing
- built-up roofing
- insulation
- cant strip
- metal deck – see structural
- steel beam – see structural
- steel post – see structural

DB-3-1   12"

DB-3-1   12"

DB-3-1   12"

top of parapet
elev. = 472'-9"

top of parapet
elev. = 472'-9"

top of parapet
elev. = 472'-9"

soffit system
- 3"x 3"x ¼" steel angle
- drip edge
- batt insulation
- 3⅝" 20 ga metal studs at 16" o.c. maximum
- ⅝" exterior gypsum board
- suspended acoustical ceiling

suspended acoustical ceiling

suspended acoustical ceiling

wall system
see wall section 1, sheet A-9 for notes

wall system
- 2x4 kiln-dried wood blocking
- ¾" exterior grade plywood
- fill void with grout
- vapor barrier
- 6" steel studs – see struct.
- 3⅝" 20 ga. metal studs at 16" o.c. maximum w/ ⅝" gyp. bd.
- 3"x 3"x ¼" steel angle
- 3½" concrete on 1½" metal deck – see structural
- steel joist – see structural
- steel beam – see structural
- 3⅝" brick and masonry ties
- 6" batt insulation
- ½" gypsum sheathing
- 3"x 3"x ¼" steel angle
- drip edge
- ⅝" exterior gypsum board
- 3⅝" 20 ga metal studs at 16" o.c. maximum

second level
elev. = 457'-4"

second level
elev. = 457'-4"

second level
elev. = 457'-4"

wall system
see wall section 1, sheet A-9 for notes

column beyond

aluminum window frame with 1" insulating glass

aluminum window frame with 1" insulating glass

aluminum window frame with 1" insulating glass

slab on grade system
see wall section 1, sheet A-9 for notes

slab on grade system
see wall section 1, sheet A-9 for notes

slab on grade system
- base and floor finish – see finish schedule
- concrete slab – see struct.
- gravel – see structural
- vapor barrier
- concrete foundation – see structural
- perimeter drain with gravel
- void form – see structural
- caisson beyond – see struct.

first level
elev. = 445'-3"

first level
elev. = 445'-3"

first level
elev. = 445'-3"

SECTION
0 0.5 1   2   4

2 SECTION
0 0.5 1   2   4

1 SECTION
0 0.5 1   2   4

A
SPECULATIVE
OFFICE
BUILDING
in
DUGONE COUNTY
for
NICHOLAS
PROPERTIES

GENW, PC.
architect
BUILDINGS R US
engineers

ISSUE:

DATE:

WALL SECTIONS

A-9

119

■ The Completed Wall Sections

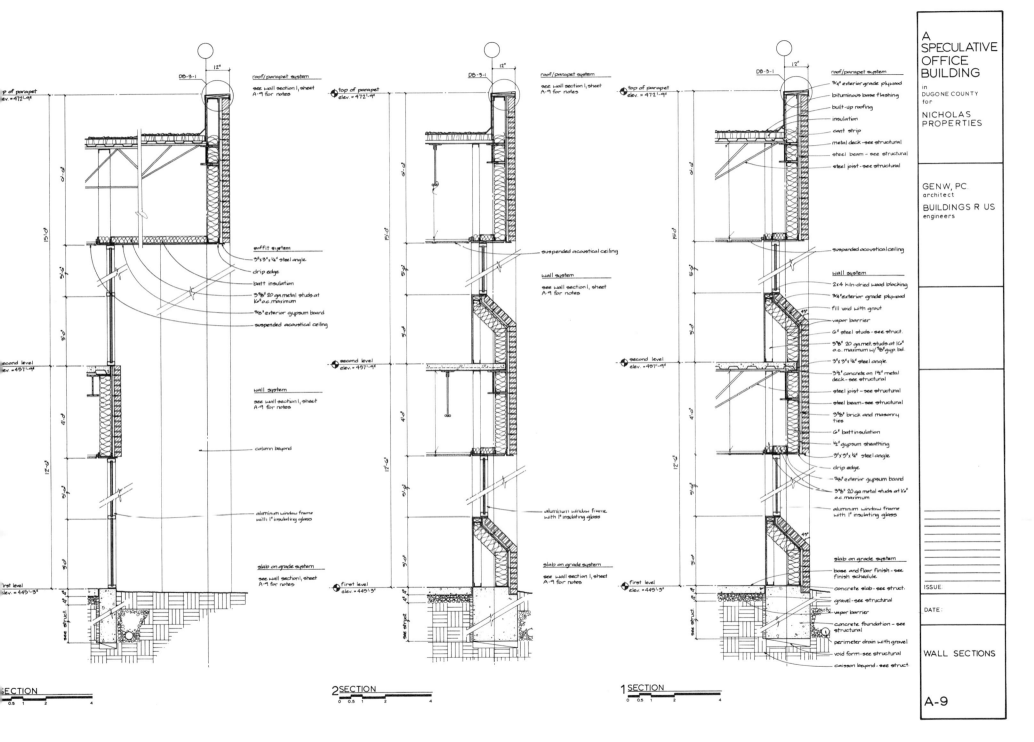

Section 3 (left) labels

roof/parapet system
see wall section 1, sheet A-9 for notes

top of parapet
elev. = 472'-9"

soffit system
5"x3"x¼" steel angle
drip edge
batt insulation
3⅝" 20 ga. metal studs at 16" o.c. maximum
⅝" exterior gypsum board
suspended acoustical ceiling

second level
elev. = 457'-9"

wall system
see wall section 1, sheet A-9 for notes

column beyond

aluminum window frame with 1" insulating glass

slab on grade system
see wall section 1, sheet A-9 for notes

first level
elev. = 445'-3"

see struct. 4'-0"

12" (DB-3-1)

Section 2 (middle) labels

top of parapet
elev. = 472'-9"

roof/parapet system
see wall section 1, sheet A-9 for notes

suspended acoustical ceiling

wall system
see wall section 1, sheet A-9 for notes

second level
elev. = 457'-9"

aluminum window frame with 1" insulating glass

slab on grade system
see wall section 1, sheet A-9 for notes

first level
elev. = 445'-3"

12" (DB-3-1)

Section 1 (right) labels

top of parapet
elev. = 472'-9"

roof/parapet system
¾" exterior grade plywood
bituminous base flashing
built-up roofing
insulation
cant strip
metal deck - see structural
steel beam - see structural
steel joist - see structural

suspended acoustical ceiling

wall system
2x4 kiln-dried wood blocking
¾" exterior grade plywood
fill void with grout
vapor barrier
6" steel studs - see struct.
3⅝" 20 ga. met. studs at 16" o.c. maximum w/ ⅝" gyp. bd.
3"x3"x¼" steel angle
3¼" concrete on 1½" metal deck - see structural
steel joist - see structural
steel beam - see structural
3⅝" brick and masonry ties
6" batt insulation
½" gypsum sheathing
3"x5"x¼" steel angle
drip edge
⅝" exterior gypsum board
3⅝" 20 ga metal studs at 16" o.c. maximum

aluminum window frame with 1" insulating glass

second level
elev. = 457'-9"

slab on grade system
base and floor finish - see finish schedule
concrete slab - see struct.
gravel - see structural
vapor barrier
concrete foundation - see structural
perimeter drain with gravel
void form - see structural
caisson beyond - see struct.

first level
elev. = 445'-3"

see struct. 4'-0"

12" (DB-3-1)

SECTION
0 0.5 1 2 4

2 SECTION
0 0.5 1 2 4

1 SECTION
0 0.5 1 2 4

Title block

A SPECULATIVE OFFICE BUILDING
in DUGONE COUNTY
for
NICHOLAS PROPERTIES

GENW, PC.
architect

BUILDINGS R US
engineers

ISSUE:

DATE:

WALL SECTIONS

A-9

9 Vertical Transportation

Vertical transportation is an all-encompassing term that is used to describe any of the elements of a building that provide access between different levels. This can include stairs, elevators, escalators, and other miscellaneous features such as ramps or ladders that might have been too large to include in the detail book.

◾ General Information

Elements of vertical transportation that occur in any given project should be drafted in both plan and section form. The plans, which are drafted at a smaller scale on the floor plans, are blown up for vertical transportation drawings to allow a higher degree of detail. Although numerous scales will work for these enlarged plans and sections, $\frac{1}{4}'' = 1'-0''$ is a good standard to use.

Elements of vertical transportation should be grouped together into similar elements when they are drafted. For example, stair plans should be drafted in a grouping with the section through the stairs. It is not uncommon for vertical transportation elements to require several sheets of construction documents. On smaller scale jobs, however, all of the elements may fit on one sheet.

Vertical transportation documents are typically started after the first phase of the floor plans has been completed. It is assumed, however, that the configuration of vertical transportation elements was calculated during the design phase of the project. Thus, in the construction documentation phase, you will already know how the sizes of the rise and run of a stair have been designed. It is also assumed that all building code requirements have been thoroughly researched and taken into account in the design of the vertical transportation elements. Building codes will dictate ranges for many elements including, but not limited to, rise and run of stairs and heights and spacing of handrails and guardrails.

Because each vertical transportation element will have its own set of guidelines, the elements have been broken down into three categories of information. Stairs are reviewed first, followed by elevators and then escalators. Graphic information, notes, and symbols can be combined for all of the elements, as these are shared standards.

Stairs

As mentioned previously, documentation for stairs will require a drawing of a stair section as well as a plan of the stair. These elements, which should cross-reference each other, will be supplemented by details in the detail book. When two or more stairs of identical design and detail occur in a building, only one needs to be drawn. The other can be noted as "similar."

Stairs may be built out of many different materials using various construction methods. In commercial work, however, concrete stairs, steel stairs with concrete-filled pans, and steel plate stairs represent the three primary methods of construction; other stairs are often built from prefabricated systems.

Concrete stairs are typically detailed extensively by the structural consultant. This relieves the architect of much of the technical detailing of the stairs themselves, leaving the drafting of profiles as the major work to be done. Concrete stairs, which provide a very solid feeling when walked upon, may be cast on or off the site. These stairs are also very quiet, making them ideal for areas where excessive foot noise would be undesirable.

Steel stairs with concrete-filled pans are easy stairs to fabricate on site and are relatively inexpensive. The architect will be expected to provide profiles as well as most of the detailing for these stairs. It will be critical, however, that the architect obtain the final sizing of all steel members from the structural consultant. This system of stair construction has almost the same feeling of solidity underfoot as that of the concrete stair. It is, however, a somewhat noisier stair system with regard to foot traffic. Still, with proper finishes this stair system can be applied to most design solutions. It is a very common method of stair construction for commercial construction and is the system that is used in the example illustrated in this book.

Steel plate stairs are inexpensive and easy to fabricate. The architect should provide the same level of detail for this system as for concrete-filled-pan stairs. This system of stair construction has the least solid feeling of solidity underfoot. It is also the noisiest system. Still, in areas that are not acoustically connected to public spaces and where aesthetics are not a concern, this system of construction may provide the best solution.

Plans must be drafted for every level of the stair that cannot be referenced to a similar condition already drafted in the set. Thus, you will always need to draft at least two plans on any stair—one for its top and one for its bottom. On stairs that are located in buildings over two stories high, there will also be an intermediate level plan. This increases the number of plans to three. If all of the intermediate level stair plans are the same on a mid- or high-rise building, the note "similar" may be used to describe all of the identical intermediate plans, and the total number of plans will remain at three. If, however, a type of intermediate plan exists that is different from the one already drafted, then it will also need to be added to the set.

Plans should be completely dimensioned and should be referenced to a column centerline when possible. They should show stair names and numbers, doors and door numbers, handrails, guardrails,

partition types, and miscellaneous features such as ladders to the roof. The plans should also note the size and number of treads on each run of the stair as well as the direction of the run.

Sections of stairs should cut the entire length and height of the stair tower in a manner such that it appears as if the stair tower had been sliced into two halves with a knife. Only on rare occasions, such as with square stair plans that have a rise and run on each side of the square, is there a need to cut a section through the width of the stair.

Sections should be completely dimensioned and should be referenced to a column centerline when possible. All finished floor elevations should be shown, as should architectural features such as handrails, guardrails, and ladders to the roof. The sections should note the size and number of risers on each run of the stair. Structural features should be appropriately drafted and noted. Remember that for concrete stairs the architect's only responsibility is to show the profile of the stair. All structural information will be indicated on the structural documents, thus requiring a minimal amount of noting on the architectural set. On steel stairs with concrete-filled pans and steel plate stairs, however, the architect is responsible for all structural information, which requires rather extensive noting.

Elevators

Elevators will require a plan and a section to be drafted for each bank of elevators in the building. When multiple elevators share the same shaft, they may be treated as a single element. Plans and sections should be cross-referenced; they will be supplemented by details that will be included in the detail book.

The two major types of elevators are traction elevators and hydraulic elevators. Traction elevators, which are substantially more expensive than hydraulic elevators, are most typically used in mid-rise or high-rise buildings. This is primarily because of the limitations on how high a hydraulic elevator can actually go. Another consideration in selecting an elevator type is the time, or interval, that it takes for an elevator to go from one stop to the next. Traction elevators are much faster than hydraulic elevators. Another difference is that traction elevators will typically require a penthouse, while hydraulic elevators will normally require an equipment room to be located near them on the level of their lowest stop.

From a drafting standpoint there is no significant difference between these two types of systems. The major distinction between elevators is more in terms of function. Passenger elevators and freight elevators have considerably different detailing; however, the actual approach to executing the construction documents will be almost identical.

The example shown in this book is a hydraulic passenger elevator, which is typical for small- to medium-scale commercial projects. It has a standard cab design, which is available from the manufacturer's standard selections. If you wish to design a custom cab, you will need to prepare an additional construction document to show all of the cab's features. Custom cabs can be very expensive, although some architects and clients find them to be worth the additional expense.

One plan will generally be adequate to describe all of the conditions of the elevator. If, however, there is a major variance in the different levels of a plan (such as a step in the size of the shaft), then you will need to draft additional plans. You should be concerned with items that are different on the interior of the shaft rather than differences that exist on the exterior of the shaft. Differences that occur on the exterior of the shaft are not included in vertical transportation documents, and are more appropriately described elsewhere. For example, differences in elevator lobbies should be described in the enlarged plans and interior elevations (see Chapter 10).

Plans should be completely dimensioned and referenced to a column centerline when possible. Partition types should be indicated and referenced to the detail book, as should other miscellaneous details.

The section of the elevator shaft should be cut so that it passes through the doors leading into the shaft. Like the stair section, it will show information from the bottom of the pit to the top of the shaft (or penthouse if included). The sections should be completely dimensioned and referenced to a column centerline when possible. All finished floor elevations should be shown. Miscellaneous architectural elements such as pit ladders should also be drafted and referenced to the detail book.

Escalators

Information on the documentation of escalators is not included in this book as it is typically supplied by the manufacturer. Frequently there will be little or no drawing that must be done to document them properly. From an architectural standpoint, your major concern will be with the detailing that occurs at the top and bottom of the run.

■ Appropriate Notes and Symbols

Finished floor elevations should be clearly labeled with a bullet. On plans, the bullet should be included as a note on the plan itself. On sections, the bullet should be drafted on the right-hand side of the section, around one inch from the actual drawing.

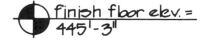

Dimensions should be in generally continuous strings, with short strings avoided. Where a dimension string intersects a column centerline, the intersection should be marked with a dot. Where a dimension string intersects any other feature, that intersection should be marked with a slash drawn at a 45-degree angle. The slash should slope from left to right for vertical dimensions and from right to left for horizontal dimensions.

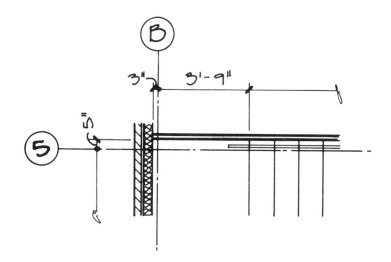

Column centerlines and column designation bubbles should be drafted in such a way that the centerline runs through the entire plan

or section. The column centerlines form the basic reference point for all dimension lines. The centerline bubble should be drafted in a size that is appropriate for the designation that needs to be labeled within it. Once a bubble size has been established, all bubbles should be drawn that same size. On plans, bubbles should be located at the top of the plan for the horizontal dimensions and to the right-hand side for vertical dimensions. On sections, bubbles should be shown at the top of the drawing. Bubbles should be drawn several inches from drawings to allow room for dimension lines.

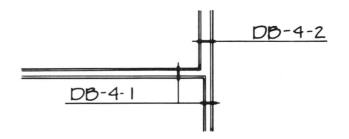

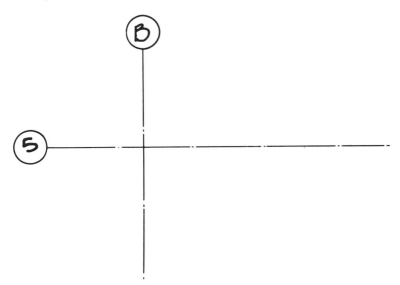

Partition type detail cuts are drafted as a short line with a slightly thickened section at the point of intersection with the wall. Above the line is placed a number that refers to the partition type in the detail book. The letters "DB" indicate that the marked detail is included in the detail book; the first number refers to the section or chapter of the detail book that contains the detail, and the second number refers to the detail number within the specified section or chapter.

Door types are indicated by a number in an ellipse shape in or near the door swing. The number in the ellipse indicates the room in which the door occurs. The letter following the number represents the particular door within the given room (see Chapter 11). The size of the ellipse should be adequate to provide for a clear labeling of all needed information. Once a size is selected, all ellipses should adhere to the standard.

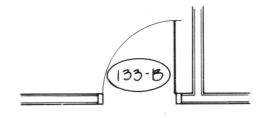

Room names and numbers should be shown in slightly larger and bolder lettering than standard. Every room should receive the same name and number that it received on the floor plans. If a room name and number will not fit into the room itself, they should be located close to the room with a leader referencing them appropriately.

Other features that should be shown on the vertical transportation documents would include ladders that lead to the roof, elevator pit ladders, handrails, and guardrails. All architectural details should be referenced to the detail book by either a cut arrow with a reference number or a reference circle with a reference number.

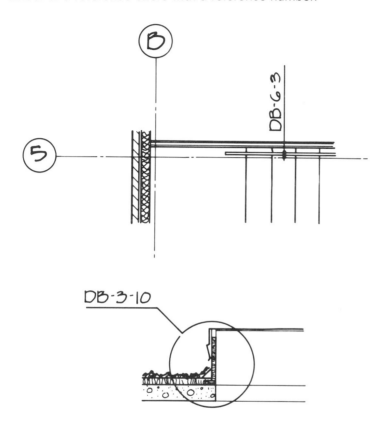

All materials should be properly indicated in accordance with the standards described in Chapter 1.

■ Sequence of the Documentation Procedure

Information that you need to draw the elements of vertical transportation is typically available early in the process of construction documentation. For this reason vertical transportation documents are usually started immediately after Phase I of the floor plans has been completed. Thus, the descriptions of vertical transportation begin with Phase II.

Phase I

Not used.

■ Phase II

As always, in the initial phase of any drawing the goal is to get as much information as possible drafted onto the sheet. This is particularly easy to do in the case of vertical transportation, where there are no major assumptions that need to be made in order to execute the document with the possible exception of the exact partition construction. Generally, however, this information should be in the process of being generated when you are drawing the vertical transportation document.

Because there are so many different elements to a vertical transportation document, you may wish to confirm your initial mock-up sheet by blocking out all of the information that will be drafted onto the sheet. In doing the block-out, lightly draft boxes where you anticipate the various drawings will be located. You then can proceed to fill in the information.

In this phase you draft the plans for the stair and the elevator and attempt to dimension them as completely as possible. Although sections are not drafted at this time, you should indicate the locations where you plan to draw them.

From a sequencing perspective, it is best, when drafting these plans, to first draw the column centerlines and label the column bubbles. In so doing, you will establish a consistent reference system for the drafting. It is an easy process to then add walls, interior features, and dimensions. This phase of the drafting is complete when the drawing has been given its title and scale, and information in the title block has been filled in properly.

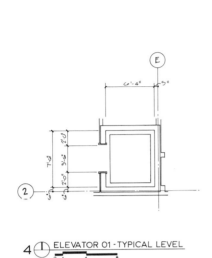

4 ⊕ ELEVATOR 01 - TYPICAL LEVEL

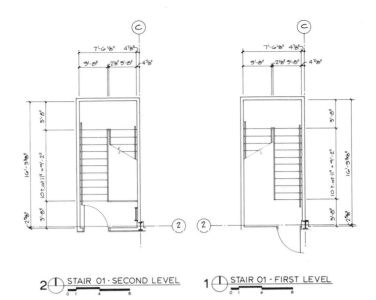

2 ⊕ STAIR 01 - SECOND LEVEL

1 ⊕ STAIR 01 - FIRST LEVEL

A
SPECULATIVE
OFFICE
BUILDING
in
DUGONE COUNTY
for

NICHOLAS
PROPERTIES

GEN W, PC.
architect

BUILDINGS R US
engineers

ISSUE:

DATE:

VERTICAL
TRANSPORTATION

A-10

■ Phase III

In the next phase of the documentation for vertical transportation, section drawings for the stairs and the elevator are added. All cross-referencing between plans and sections is also indicated.

Drafting stair sections, while not difficult, is very time-consuming. The addition of these drawings to the sheet represents a substantial amount of work.

From a sequencing perspective, it is best, when drafting these sections, to first draw the column centerline, column bubbles, and the finish floor elevations. With these lines established, it will be much easier to fill in the required information.

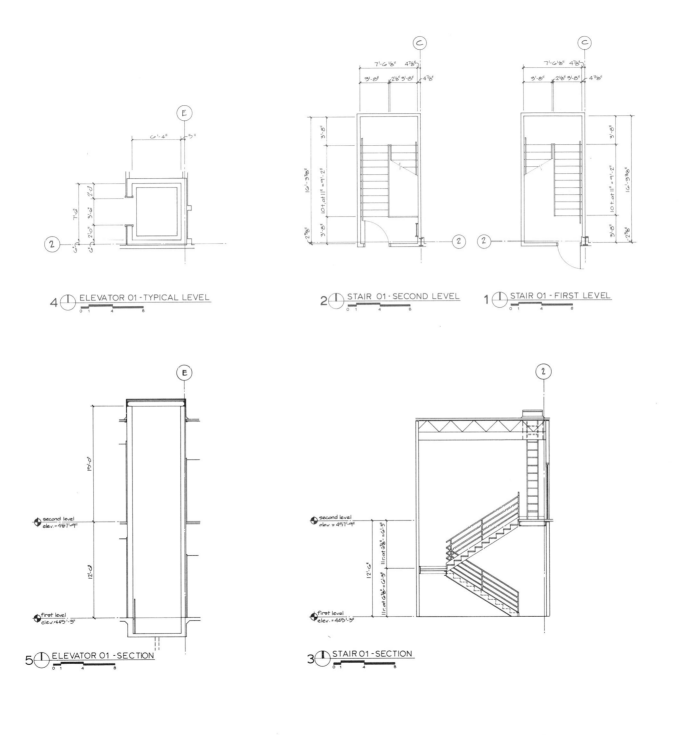

4 — ELEVATOR 01 - TYPICAL LEVEL
0 1   4   8

2 — STAIR 01 · SECOND LEVEL
0 1   4   8

1 — STAIR 01 - FIRST LEVEL
0 1   4   8

5 — ELEVATOR 01 - SECTION
0 1   4   8

3 — STAIR 01 - SECTION
0 1   4   8

second level
elev. = 457'-9"

first level
elev. = 445'-3"

A
SPECULATIVE
OFFICE
BUILDING
IN
DUGONE COUNTY
for

NICHOLAS
PROPERTIES

GEN W, PC
architect

BUILDINGS R US
engineers

ISSUE:

DATE:

VERTICAL
TRANSPORTATION

A - 10

■ Phase IV

During the final phase of the documentation for vertical transportation, all of the miscellaneous notes and references to the detail book that were not done previously are added to the document sheet.

At this stage, room names and numbers should be copied from the floor plan onto the sheet and doors should be given their reference numbers. Partitions types, which will be complete at this point in the process, should have their references added to the plan as well.

Material indications, although not essential for the vertical transportation construction documents, are helpful in making the drawings easier for others to understand. They may be added at this stage. Most important during this phase, however, is the addition of miscellaneous notes. Frequently you will not have had time to draft an item that might have been desirable to have included in the documents. In these cases it is important to at least note the item. In so doing you ensure that the item will not be overlooked during the bid process of the project.

It is also appropriate to check your work at this phase of the documentation. Verify all cross-references, detail references, and dimension strings.

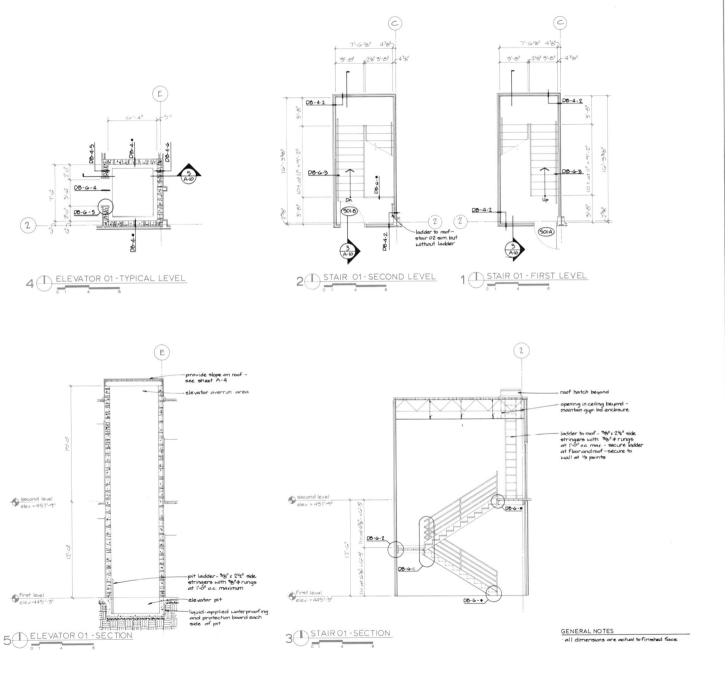

4 ELEVATOR 01 - TYPICAL LEVEL
0 1 4 8

2 STAIR 01 - SECOND LEVEL
0 1 4 8

1 STAIR 01 - FIRST LEVEL
0 1 4 8

ladder to roof - stair 02 sim. but without ladder

5 ELEVATOR 01 - SECTION
0 1 4 8

provide slope on roof - see sheet A-4

elevator overrun area

second level elev. = 457'-9"

first level elev. = 445'-3"

pit ladder - 3/8" x 2 1/2" side stringers with 3/8" ø rungs at 1'-0" o.c. maximum

elevator pit

liquid-applied waterproofing and protection board each side of pit

3 STAIR 01 - SECTION

roof hatch beyond

opening in ceiling beyond - maintain gyp. bd. enclosure

ladder to roof - 3/8" x 2 1/2" side stringers with 3/8" ø rungs at 1'-0" o.c. max. - secure ladder at floor and roof - secure to wall at 1/3 points

second level elev. = 457'-9"

first level elev. = 445'-3"

GENERAL NOTES
· all dimensions are actual to finished face

A SPECULATIVE OFFICE BUILDING

in DUGONE COUNTY
for

NICHOLAS PROPERTIES

GEN W, PC
architect

BUILDINGS R US
engineers

ISSUE

DATE:

VERTICAL TRANSPORTATION

A - 10

133

■ The Completed Vertical Transportation

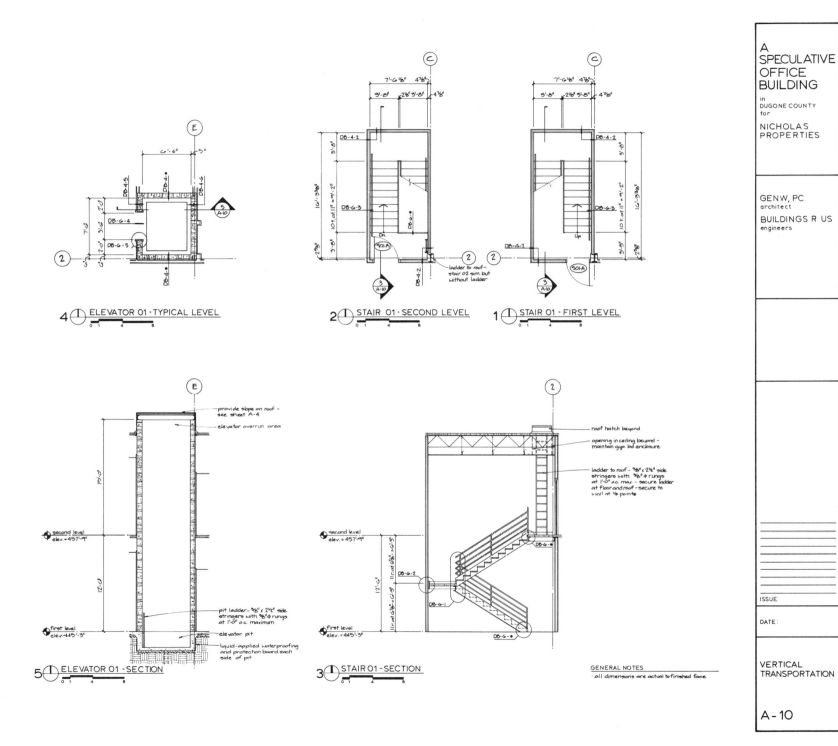

4 ⊕ ELEVATOR 01 - TYPICAL LEVEL
  0 1   4   8

2 ⊕ STAIR 01 - SECOND LEVEL
  0 1   4   8

1 ⊕ STAIR 01 - FIRST LEVEL
  0 1   4   8

ladder to roof —
stair 02 sim. but
without ladder

provide slope on roof —
see sheet A-4

elevator overrun area

roof hatch beyond

opening in ceiling beyond —
maintain gyp. bd enclosure.

ladder to roof - 3/8" x 2½" side
stringers with 3/8" ⌀ rungs
at 1'-0" o.c. max. - secure ladder
at floor and roof - secure to
wall at ⅓ points

second level
elev. = 457'-9"

first level
elev. = 445'-3"

second level
elev. = 457'-9"

first level
elev. = 445'-3"

pit ladder - 3/8" x 2½" side
stringers with 3/8" ⌀ rungs
at 1'-0" o.c. maximum

elevator pit

liquid-applied waterproofing
and protection board each
side of pit

5 ⊕ ELEVATOR 01 - SECTION
  0 1   4   8

3 ⊕ STAIR 01 - SECTION
  0 1   4   8

GENERAL NOTES
· all dimensions are actual to finished face

A
SPECULATIVE
OFFICE
BUILDING
in
DUGONE COUNTY
for
NICHOLAS
PROPERTIES

GENW, PC.
architect
BUILDINGS R US
engineers

ISSUE:

DATE:

VERTICAL
TRANSPORTATION

A-10

10 Enlarged Plans and Interior Elevations

Enlarged plans and interior elevations are typically shown for areas where the architect wishes to exercise extensive design control. Enlarged plans are drafted in order to show a greater amount of detail than can be seen in the smaller scale floor plans. Interior elevations are drafted to provide a detailed view of how an interior wall and the features of that wall should be built.

Enlarged plans do not necessarily require that interior elevations be drawn to accompany them. Similarly, interior elevations do not necessarily need to be referenced to enlarged plans, as they may also be referenced from the smaller scale floor plans. Typically, however, the two drawings will be done together.

■ General Information

Areas that are frequently "blown up" for enlarged plans and interior elevations include toilet rooms, kitchens, lobbies, and other highly detailed spaces where a larger scale might be necessary to convey a complete understanding of the design intent. Stairs and elevators are also blown up as enlarged plans, but are typically shown as separate elements (see Chapter 9).

Enlarged plans and interior elevations are usually started after the first phase of the floor plans has been completed. When drafting an enlarged plan, you should imagine looking down at a floor after the building has been sliced several feet above the finished floor being referenced. You see the tops of casework, plumbing fixtures, and other interior features, as well as sections through exterior walls, interior partitions, and the structure. Interior elevations are drafted as if you were facing a wall that is several feet in front of you.

Enlarged plans and interior elevations should be drafted at a scale that allows a detailed presentation of all of the required information. The most common scales are $\frac{1}{4}'' = 1'$-$0''$ and $\frac{1}{2}'' = 1'$-$0''$. Interior elevations are typically shown at the same scale as the enlarged plans. This helps to provide a more consistent and easily understood document.

Enlarged plans should always be oriented on a sheet in the same manner as the smaller scale floor plans. If there is only one enlarged plan, it should be located in the upper right-hand corner of the sheet. If there are two or more plans, they should be located along the top of the sheet. When possible, interior elevations should be located adjacent to the enlarged plan from which they are referenced.

The convention in drafting the interior elevations is to first draw an elevation of the space that has the lowest sequenced room number on the plan, then continue with the other spaces in ascending order. The north elevation in a space should always be elevated first, with other walls following in a clockwise direction. If you do not feel the need to elevate every wall in a space, it is acceptable to skip certain elevations. There is also no requirement for each space on a plan to be elevated. The primary guideline should be control. If you want absolute control over some element of a wall, you should elevate it. Most walls, however, will not require this degree of control.

When composing the layout for enlarged plans and interior elevations you should be aware that these elements commonly require several sheets of construction documents. It is best, therefore, to group like plans and elevations when there is enough information to require multiple sheets. For example, enlarged plans and interior elevations for toilet rooms may be drawn on one sheet and enlarged plans and interior elevations for the building lobby on a second sheet.

Enlarged plans typically use framing dimensions, although on occasion actual dimensions may be more appropriate. The decision should be based on the intent of the plan. If the plan has been enlarged because a level of complexity exists that cannot be properly indicated on a smaller scale plan, and finishes are not of primary importance, the framing system of dimensions will be appropriate. If, however, the plan has been enlarged in order to provide a greater definition of finish materials, the "actual" system of dimensioning will be more appropriate. The example in this book uses framing dimensions. (See Chapter 3 for a more complete description of the various methods of indicating dimensions on plans.)

Because of the nature of the information they are intended to convey, interior elevations always use "actual" dimensions. Interior elevations are drawn primarily to give the architect increased control over the placement of interior elements. Thus, the "actual" dimension system relates more to the intent of the drawing.

■ Appropriate Notes and Symbols

Finished floor elevations on enlarged plans should be clearly labeled with a bullet. All level changes that take place on a given plan should be indicated. Ramp elevation changes should be shown in feet and inches with spot elevations.

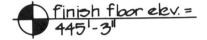

Dimensions should be in generally continuous strings. Short strings should be avoided. Where a dimension string intersects a column centerline, the intersection should be marked with a dot. Where a dimension string intersects any other feature, that intersection should be marked with a slash drawn at a 45-degree angle. The slash should slope from left to right for vertical dimensions and from right to left for horizontal dimensions.

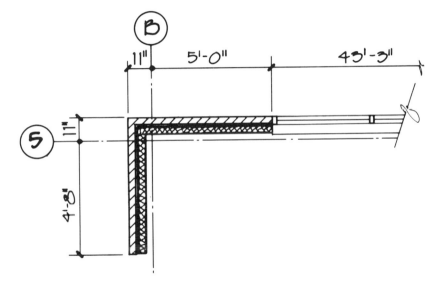

Column centerlines and column designation bubbles should be drafted in such a way that the centerline runs through the entire enlarged plan. Drafted as a series of long lines with single dashes, the column centerlines form the basic reference point for all dimension lines. The size of the centerline bubble should be appropriate for the designation to be labeled within it. All bubbles should be the same size and should be located at the top of the enlarged plan for horizontal dimensions and to the right-hand side of the enlarged plan for vertical dimensions. Bubbles should always be drafted several inches from the enlarged plan to allow space for dimension lines. Interior elevations will not need to include column centerline references.

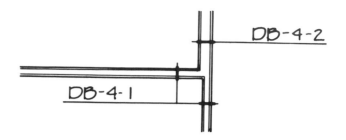

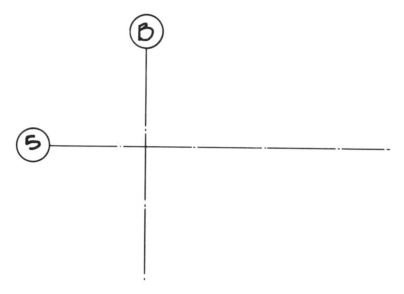

Partition type detail cuts are drawn as a short line with a slightly thickened section at the point of intersection with the wall. Above the line is placed a number that refers to the partition type in the detail book. The letters "DB" indicate that the marked detail is included in the detail book; the first number refers to the section or chapter of the detail book that contains the detail, and the second number refers to the detail number within the specified section or chapter.

Cross-referencing cuts—wall sections. The arrow symbol shown below refers to a wall section that is located on another sheet within the set of construction documents. Underneath the arrow is a number to help locate the section. The first number refers to the sheet number, while the second number refers to the particular drawing on the sheet. The size of the arrowhead is not critical, although once a size has been selected, it should be held consistent. A good system for drawing arrows is to make the bottom of the arrow a minimum of ⅜″ and to draw the sides with the 30-degree side of a 30/60 triangle.

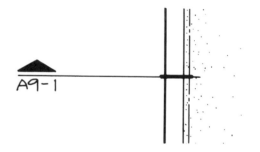

Cross-referencing cuts—elevation. The next symbol shown refers to an interior elevation that is located either on the same sheet or on another sheet within the set of construction documents. The bottom number refers to the sheet number, and the top number to the particular drawing on that sheet. The size of the circle should be such that it can easily contain the information that is labeled inside of it. Once a size is selected, all circles should adhere to that standard.

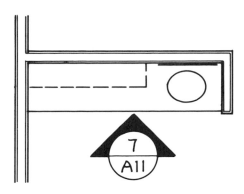

Room names and numbers should be drafted in lettering that is slightly larger and bolder than standard. Every room should receive the same name and number that it received on the floor plans. If a room name and number will not fit into the room itself, they should be located near the room with a leader referencing them appropriately.

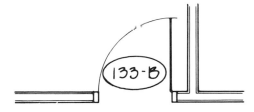

Door types are indicated by a number in an ellipse shape in or near the door swing. The number in the ellipse indicates the room number in which the door occurs. The letter following the number represents the particular door within the given room (see Chapter 11). The size of the ellipse should be adequate to provide for a clear labeling of all needed information. Once a size is selected, all ellipses should adhere to the standard.

In a room where changes in floor finishes occur, they should be drawn and noted. The division should be indicated with an "X" arrowhead and the immediate area at the division should be rendered appropriately (see page 13 for information on material indications). Changes in floor finishes need not be indicated graphically when the changes occur at door openings.

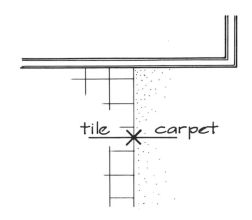

Other features that should be drawn on the enlarged plans and interior elevations might include casework, floor drains, plumbing fixtures, floor mats, and structural columns. All architectural details should be referenced to the detail book by either a cut arrow with a reference number or a reference circle with a reference number.

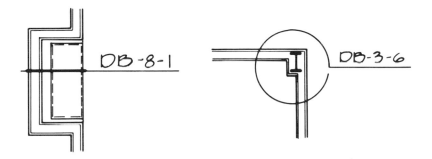

All materials should be properly indicated in accordance with the standards described in Chapter 1.

■ **Sequence of the Documentation Procedure**
Because enlarged plans and interior elevations key off of the smaller scale floor plans, they are usually not started until Phase II. When they are started, it is typical to draw the plans ahead of the elevations.

Phase I
Not used.

■ Phase II

In executing the documentation for enlarged plans and interior elevations, the first step should be to block out all of the required information. This requires you to decide which interior elevations to draw. Although this decision can always be changed, you should make a serious attempt to make the block-out complete.

After the block-out is complete, the next step is to draft the enlarged plan(s). This drafting of the plans should be virtually complete before any work is started on the interior elevations. Drafting the enlarged plans is usually relatively easy since the basic information required to execute them will have already been shown on the floor plans.

From a sequencing perspective, it is best, when drafting these plans, to first draft the column centerlines and label the column bubbles. In so doing, you establish a basic reference system for the drafting. Any structural elements should also be drawn at this time. Next, walls can be drafted, followed by plumbing fixtures and toilet partitions. Finally, you should add dimensions that are as complete as possible. Complete this phase of the drafting by giving the drawings their titles and scales and filling in the complete information for the title block.

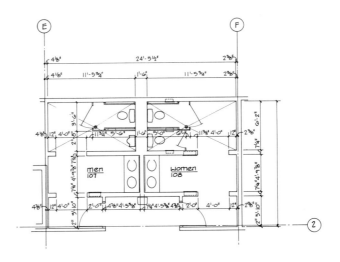

1 ENLARGED FLOOR PLAN

A
SPECULATIVE
OFFICE
BUILDING
in
DUGONE COUNTY
for

NICHOLAS
PROPERTIES

GENW, PC.
architect

BUILDINGS R US
engineers

ISSUE:

DATE:

ENLARGED
PLANS AND
INTERIOR
ELEVATIONS

A - 11

■ Phase III

In this phase of the documentation for the enlarged plans and interior elevations, all of the interior elevations are drafted. To draft these elevations, however, requires the selection of any feature that will be located on the wall and, therefore, on the drawings. In the drawing in this book, for example, all of the toilet accessories were selected and drafted.

In selecting accessories it is important to note the manufacturer's recommended mounting heights. These heights are then noted on the interior elevations, which is important if the architect wishes to have control over the precise locations of accessories. It is also important in the selection of accessories to verify that the thickness of the partition is adequate to receive any accessories that are intended to be recessed into it. During the construction phase of a project, it is not uncommon to discover that a specified toilet accessory will not fit into the partition where it was intended. A good guideline for partitions that will have accessories recessed into them is to provide a clear space in the partition of at least six inches. You should also verify that the mounting heights and locations of accessories meet the requirements of the applicable codes and ANSI standards.

In this phase you also add the cross-referencing for various elements of the project. Partition type references and interior elevation references are added.

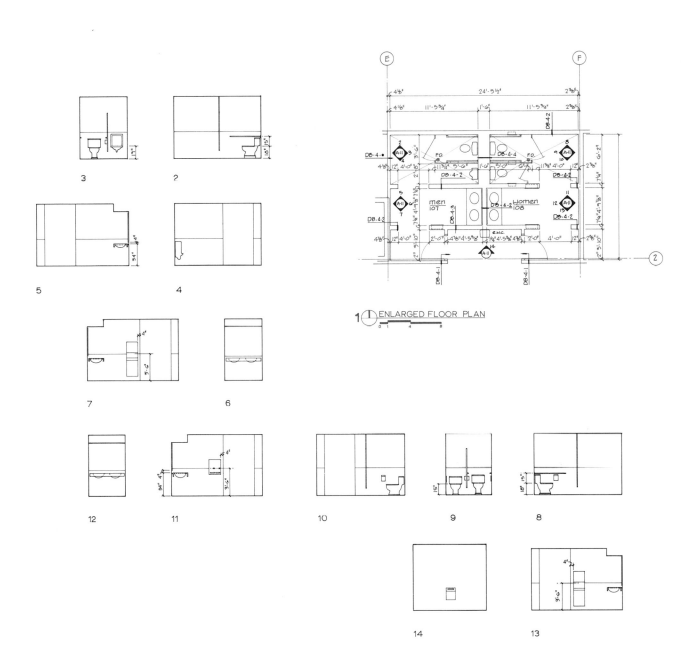

1 ⟶ ENLARGED FLOOR PLAN

3   2

5   4

7   6

12   11   10   9   8

14   13

A
SPECULATIVE
OFFICE
BUILDING
in
DUGONE COUNTY
for

NICHOLAS
PROPERTIES

GEN W, PC
architect

BUILDINGS R US
engineers

ISSUE:

DATE:

ENLARGED
PLANS AND
INTERIOR
ELEVATIONS

A-11

■ Phase IV

The final phase of the documentation for the enlarged plans and interior elevations reflects the addition of all remaining cross-referencing and miscellaneous notes. Miscellaneous notes are intended to describe any element of the drawing that is important to the project but for some reason has not been included in the detailing.

Material indications are added to the document in this phase. As with floor plans, it is not essential that material indications be added to the enlarged plans. It is essential, however, that material indications be added to the interior elevations. By providing this graphic reinforcement to the drawing, you assure that the drawing is as clear as possible.

All work should be checked during this final phase. Dimensions, cross-referencing, and detail references should all be verified.

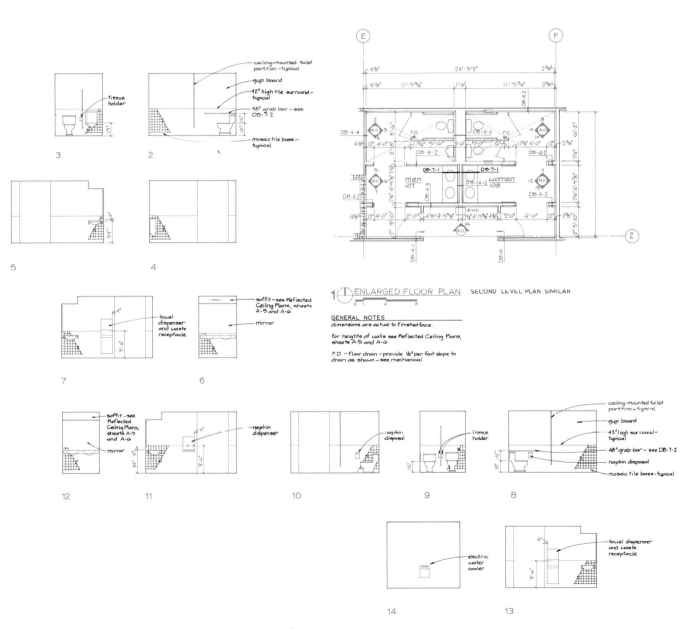

ceiling-mounted toilet partition—typical

tissue holder

gyp. board

42" high tile surround—typical

48" grab bar — see DB-7-2

mosaic tile base — typical

3

2

5

4

soffit—see Reflected Ceiling Plans, sheets A-5 and A-6

mirror

towel dispenser and waste receptacle

7

6

soffit—see Reflected Ceiling Plans, sheets A-5 and A-6

napkin dispenser

napkin disposal

tissue holder

ceiling-mounted toilet partition—typical

gyp. board

42" high surround—typical

48" grab bar — see DB-7-2

napkin disposal

mosaic tile base—typical

mirror

napkin holder

12

11

10

9

8

electric water cooler

towel dispenser and waste receptacle

14

13

men 107

women 108

1 ENLARGED FLOOR PLAN   SECOND LEVEL PLAN SIMILAR

0 1   4   8

GENERAL NOTES

dimensions are actual to finished face.

for heights of walls see Reflected Ceiling Plans, sheets A-5 and A-6.

F.D. — floor drain — provide 1/8" per foot slope to drain as shown — see mechanical.

A
SPECULATIVE
OFFICE
BUILDING

in
DUGONE COUNTY
for

NICHOLAS
PROPERTIES

GENW, PC
architect

BUILDINGS R US
engineers

ISSUE

DATE:

ENLARGED
PLANS AND
INTERIOR
ELEVATIONS

A - 11

■ The Completed Enlarged Plans and Interior Elevations

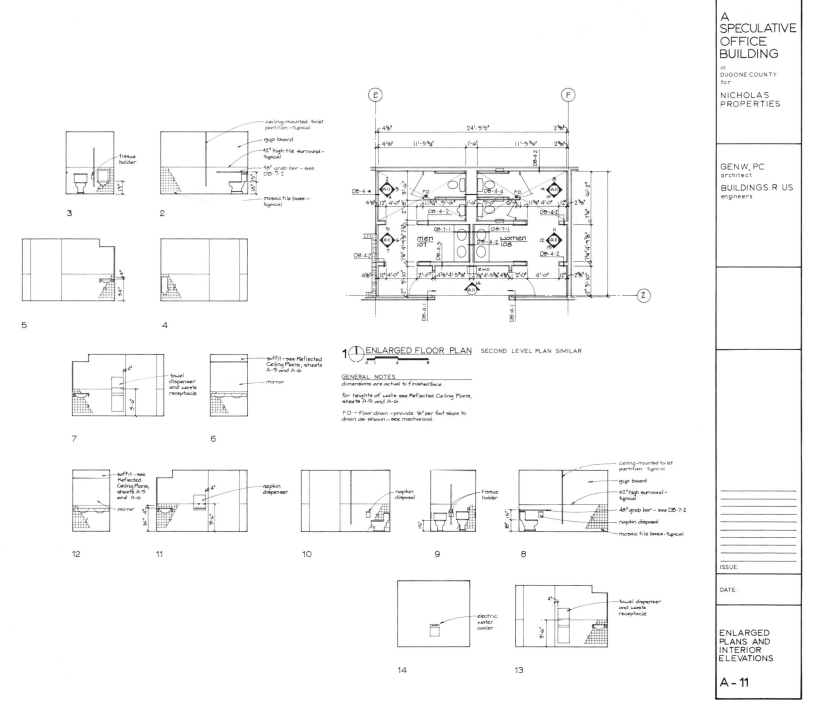

3

2

ceiling-mounted toilet
partition - typical

gyp board

42" high tile surround -
typical

48" grab bar - see
DB-7-2

mosaic tile base -
typical

tissue
holder

5

4

7

6

soffit - see Reflected
Ceiling Plans, sheets
A-5 and A-6

towel
dispenser
and waste
receptacle

mirror

E   F

4½"   24'-5½"   2¾"

4½"   11'-5¾"   1'-6"   11'-5¾"   2¾"

DB-4-2

DB-4-1

A-11

FD.   DB-4-4   FD.

A-11

DB-4-2   DB-4-2

DB-7-1   DB-7-1

men
107   DB-4-2   women
108

A-11   A-11

DB-4-2   DB-4-2

DB-4-1   DB-4-1

A-11

1 ENLARGED FLOOR PLAN   SECOND LEVEL PLAN SIMILAR

0   1   4   8

GENERAL NOTES
dimensions are actual to finished face.

for heights of walls see Reflected Ceiling Plans,
sheets A-5 and A-6.

F.O. - floor drain - provide ¼" per foot slope to
drain as shown - see mechanical.

12

11

10

9

8

soffit - see
Reflected
Ceiling Plans,
sheets A-5
and A-6

mirror

napkin
dispenser

napkin
disposal

tissue
holder

ceiling-mounted toilet
partition - typical

gyp board

42" high surround -
typical

48" grab bar - see DB-7-2

napkin disposal

mosaic tile base - typical

14

13

electric
water
cooler

towel dispenser
and waste
receptacle

A
SPECULATIVE
OFFICE
BUILDING
in
DUGONE COUNTY
for

NICHOLAS
PROPERTIES

GENW, PC
architect

BUILDINGS R US
engineers

ISSUE:

DATE:

ENLARGED
PLANS AND
INTERIOR
ELEVATIONS

A-11

11 Schedules

The term schedule is applied here rather loosely to three distinct groups of information: window frame types, door schedules, and finish schedules. Some architects prefer to put these three groups of information into the detail book, but many incorporate them into the construction document set. On smaller projects you may be able to combine all three of these elements onto one sheet of drawings. On larger jobs, however, a finish schedule alone may require several sheets of drawings. The example in this book groups them together onto one sheet.

■ General Information

Because these schedules are often drafted onto the same sheet, it is important to group them into individual areas. Each of these elements has its own unique set of requirements for proper documentation. It is appropriate, therefore, to review each of them separately. The standard presentation of the sample document is included at the end of the chapter.

■ Window Frame Types

Strictly speaking, window frame types are not actually "schedule" items. Rather, they are elevations of all of the window frames that occur in the building's exterior façade. These elevations show not only the frame elevation, but also the glass type and all of the detail cuts that are included in the detail book.

Window frame types are typically drawn at a scale of $\frac{1}{4}'' = 1'\text{-}0''$, although $\frac{1}{8}'' = 1'\text{-}0''$ or $\frac{1}{2}'' = 1'\text{-}0''$ may be appropriate for some projects. The example in this book uses a scale of $\frac{1}{4}'' = 1'\text{-}0''$.

Window frame types are referenced from the exterior elevations by means of a polygon-shaped symbol and a number. The same symbol and number should be drafted immediately under each frame elevation that is shown. Every window that is unique should receive a number; identical windows may share a number. Remember, however, that because details are referenced from these elevations, identical windows must have the exact same head, sill, and jamb conditions. The glass and glazing system for each window must also be identical. Windows that meet this criteria should be considered identical and may be given the same reference number.

In assigning numbers to the windows on the exterior elevations, you should start on the right-hand side of the north elevation, numbering each window in sequence as you move to the left. After the north elevation is complete, continue to other elevations, moving in a clockwise direction. When drafting the window frame types onto a sheet, you should follow the same order.

Appropriate Notes and Symbols

Column centerlines and column designation bubbles should be drafted in such a way that the centerline runs through the entire widow elevation. The centerline bubble should be drawn in a size that is appropriate for the designation to be labeled within it. All bubbles should be the same size and should be located at the top of the elevation. Bubbles should be drafted several inches away from the elevation to allow space for dimension lines.

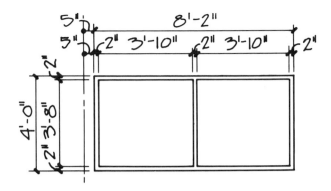

Window frame types should be indicated with a reference number placed within a pentagon or other multledged polygon. The size of the pentagon is not critical, but should be held constant for the entire set of documents.

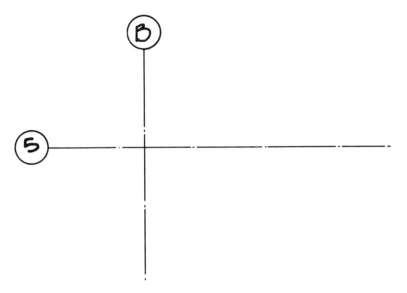

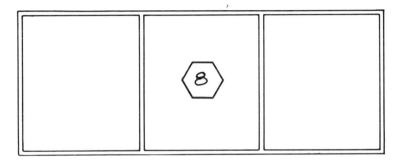

Dimensions should be in generally continuous strings. Short strings should be avoided. Where a dimension string intersects a column centerline, the intersection should be marked with a dot. Where a dimension string intersects any other feature, that intersection should be marked with a slash drawn at a 45-degree angle. The slash should slope left to right for vertical dimensions and from right to left for horizontal dimensions.

All architectural details should be referenced to the detail book by a cut arrow with a reference number.

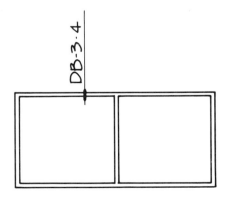

Door Schedules

The door schedule is designed to show the type of door being used in a given opening, the type of frame for the door, and the details that will be used for the door and frame. There are many ways to convey this information properly, and every architect will have a personal preference. The method included here is a hybrid of several systems.

Door schedules can be divided into three different sections: door types, frame types, and tabular information. The first section, door types, is graphic in nature. Here every type of door that exists on the particular project is shown in elevation. These elevations are typically shown at $\frac{1}{4}'' = 1'\text{-}0''$, although this scale is not a rigid standard. Any windows or other special features of the door (such as kick plates) should also be drafted, dimensionally located, and noted. Each door should receive an alphabetic designation. This designation will key into the tabular information section of the door schedule.

The second section of the door schedule, frame types, is also graphic in nature. Here every style of frame that exists on the particular project is shown in elevation and dimensioned. The frame type elevation should be shown at the same scale as the door type elevation. Each frame should receive a numeric designation, which will key into the tabular information section of the door schedule.

The third section of the door schedule is a tabular section that contains the bulk of the information about the given assembly. Included are:

1. *The door number.* This is the number that the door received on the floor plan. Each door should have its own number, even if it is identical to another. The number has two sections. For example, the number 102-A represents door "A" in room 102. This system of referencing makes the door very easy to locate on the floor plans.

2. *The door type.* This is the alphabetic designation that is given to the graphic representation of the actual door as described above.

3. *The door material.* The most common materials for doors are wood, aluminum, and hollow metal.

4. *The door width.*

5. *The door height.*

6. *The door thickness.* Although all of the doors used in the example in this book are $1\frac{3}{4}''$ thick, it is important to remember that different types of doors will have different thicknesses. Always verify thicknesses with applicable standards and manufacturer's information.

7. *The frame type.* This is the numeric designation that is given to

the graphic representation of the door frame as described above.

8. *The frame material.* The most common materials for door frames are wood, aluminum, and hollow metal.

9. *Detail references for the strike, hinge, head, and sill.* These details should be added to the detail book.

10. *The hardware group number.* Hardware groups are generally included in the project specifications. The purpose of listing the hardware group is to specify the items that will be included in a door/frame assembly. Items such as closers, hinges, locksets, and so forth are listed in terms of quantities needed per door and manufacturer. Information about hardware groups is not included in this book; it can be assembled from manufacturers' literature.

11. *Remarks.* Every schedule will always have an area in it for general remarks.

A blank copy of the tabular part of the door schedule is provided in Appendix A. The reason for filling in a door schedule is to indicate your design intent and compliance with the appropriate code. If, for example, you want a $3'\text{-}0'' \times 7'\text{-}0''$ wood door to be installed in a hollow metal frame for a particular office, all you need to do is to indicate the appropriate information on the door schedule.

Finish Schedules

The finish schedule is designed to show general room finishes. In rooms or individual walls of certain rooms with complex finishes, it will be necessary to draft an interior elevation to supplement the finish schedule (see Chapter 10). The finish schedule consists of two tabular sections: the main section, which is the schedule itself, and a second section, which is the "key," or reference section, for the main section. For example, rather than writing "water-resistant gypsum board" on the main schedule, you would give it an alphabetic designation, such as "A," and use this designation in the schedule each time that water-resistant gypsum board is called for as a material. This keying saves a tremendous amount of time and space in preparing the finish schedule.

In the key section of the schedule there will be two primary types of information that will receive designations. Materials, such as brick or gypsum board, will be given alphabetic designations. Finishes, such as paint or sealer, will be given numeric designations. These keys are simply lists that occur along with the main section of the schedule.

The main part of the finish schedule consists of a tabular form where the bulk of the information about finishes is presented. Included on the form are:

1. *The room number.* This should be copied from the floor plans. Typically the schedule will list all rooms in ascending order.

2. *The room name.* This should also be copied from the floor plans.

3. *The material and finish of the floor.* Typical floor materials would include unglazed ceramic tile. Typical finishes would include factory.

4. *The material and finish of the base.* Typical materials would include vinyl. Typical finishes would include factory.

5. *The material and finish of each wall in the room, beginning with the north elevation and proceeding in a clockwise direction.* Typical materials would include gypsum board. Typical finishes would include paint.

6. *The material and finish of the ceiling.* Typical materials would include suspended acoustical ceiling. Typical finishes would include factory.

7. *Remarks.* This area is reserved for any miscellaneous comments that might be needed to convey a complete understanding of the design intent.

A copy of a blank finish schedule with all of these categories of information is included in Appendix A. As with the door schedule, filling in a finish schedule is primarily a matter of indicating your design intent.

Although the sample schedules in the appendix have been drawn by hand, you can save a great amount of time by having them typed on a word processor. In so doing, you will always have the latest information for the schedules available for reference and editing, but will not need to draft the schedules until they are complete. Thus, you can easily incorporate any last-minute changes without disturbing your sequencing.

■ Sequence of the Documentation Procedure

Schedules are typically among the last elements to be drafted in a set of construction documents. Of the three types of schedules discussed in this chapter, window frame types should be started first, followed by the door schedule and finally the finish schedule. This is not to say that none of the information for doors and finishes is known before the end of the project. In fact, you should start preparing a preliminary list of all of the door and finish items during the design phase of the project. The main reason that the schedules are not completed until the end of the documentation process is to reduce the damage that last-minute changes can have on the fabric of the schedules. By waiting, you can be more assured that number sequences will remain constant. Thus, even though the schedules will not be filled in until the later phase of the documentation process, work on them should be started at the outset of the project's design.

Phase I
Not used.

Phase II
Not used.

■ Phase III

The most important step in starting the documentation of schedules is to do a good mock-up of all of the information that will need to be drafted onto the sheet. By estimating the number of windows that will need to be shown, you can see how much space will be required for window frame types. Also, by counting the number of rooms and doors on the floor plans, you will be able to estimate the sizes of the door and finish schedules.

These estimates are done at this phase of the drawing. The door schedule should be drafted large enough to handle 10 to 15 percent more doors than expected. The finish schedule should be drafted to handle a similar percentage of additions. Although the basic schedules are drafted at this stage, no information is noted in them yet.

Window frame types are drafted and dimensioned in this phase. References to details in the detail book are also shown. At this stage of documentation the window frame types are already complete.

The schedules are next appropriately titled and given scales as necessary. The title block is also filled in properly.

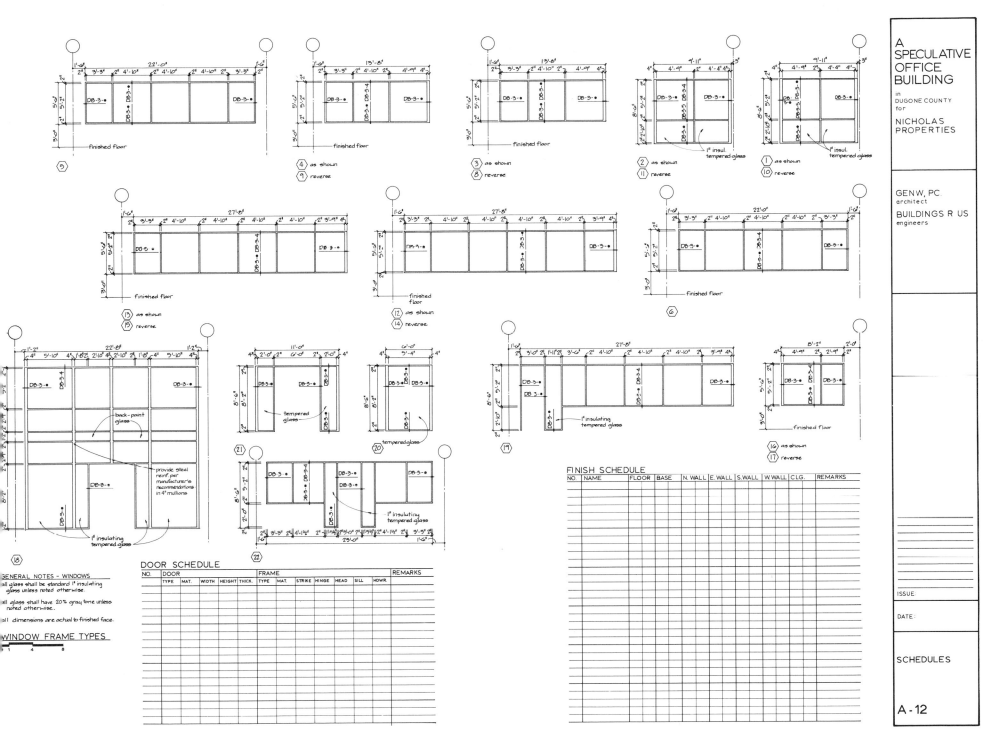

■ Phase IV

In this phase of the documentation of the schedules, all of the information for schedules is filled in. On small projects schedules are generally easy to execute. On larger projects, however, coordination and design revisions can make schedules more challenging. Note on the sample schedules that occasionally blank lines have been inserted. These blank lines are inserted to ensure that any information that might need to be added at the last minute will be provided a slot that will not be too far out of the proper sequence of numbering.

During this final phase of documentation it is appropriate to check the information on the drawings. This is particularly important for schedules, where it is very easy to transpose numbers when filling in information. In addition to verifying this information, you should also verify all detail references on the window frame types.

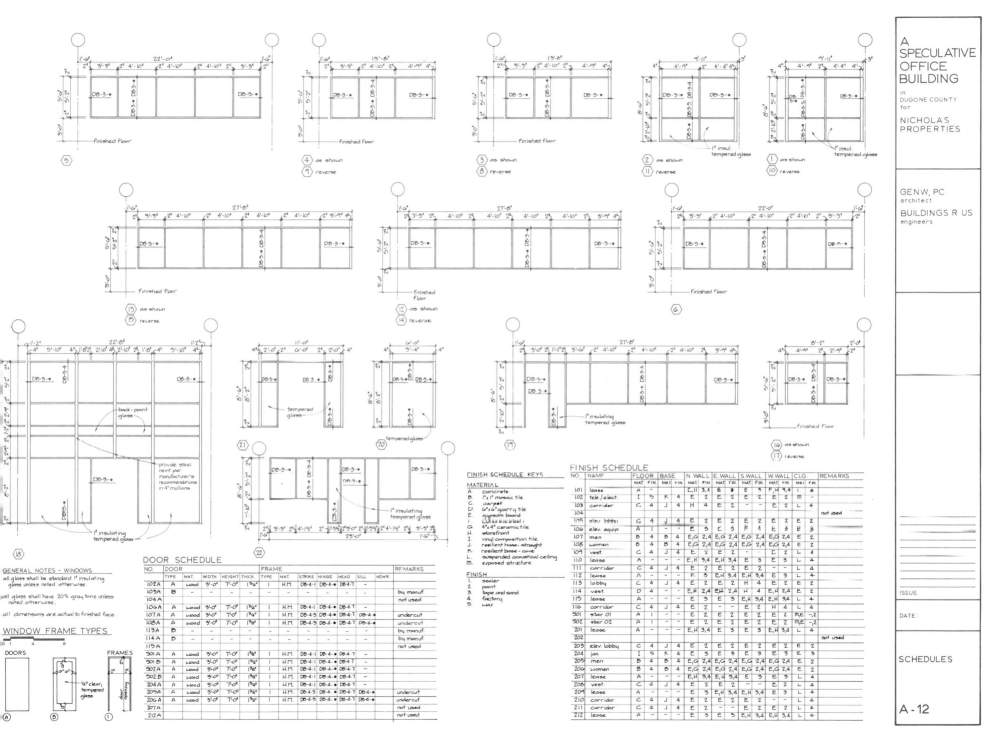

A SPECULATIVE OFFICE BUILDING

in DUGONE COUNTY for

NICHOLAS PROPERTIES

GEN W, PC
architect

BUILDINGS R US
engineers

ISSUE

DATE:

SCHEDULES

A-12

GENERAL NOTES – WINDOWS

all glass shall be standard 1" insulating glass unless noted otherwise.

all glass shall have 20% gray tone unless noted otherwise.

all dimensions are actual to finished face.

WINDOW FRAME TYPES

DOORS

FRAMES

¼" clear, tempered glass

door opening

Ⓐ Ⓓ Ⓘ

DOOR SCHEDULE

NO.	DOOR TYPE	MAT.	WIDTH	HEIGHT	THICK.	FRAME TYPE	MAT.	STRIKE	HINGE	HEAD	SILL	HDWR.	REMARKS
102A	A	wood	3'-0"	7'-0"	1¾"	I	H.M.	DB-4-1	DB-4-•	DB-4-7			
103A	B	–											by manuf.
104A													not used
106A	A	wood	3'-0"	7'-0"	1¾"	I	H.M.	DB-4-1	DB-4-•	DB-4-7			
107A	A	wood	3'-0"	7'-0"	1¾"	I	H.M.	DB-4-3	DB-4-•	DB-4-7	DB-4-•		undercut
108A	A	wood	3'-0"	7'-0"	1¾"	I	H.M.	DB-4-3	DB-4-•	DB-4-7	DB-4-•		undercut
113A	B	–											by manuf.
114A	B	–											by manuf.
115A													not used
501A	A	wood	3'-0"	7'-0"	1¾"	I	H.M.	DB-4-1	DB-4-•	DB-4-7	–		
501B	A	wood	3'-0"	7'-0"	1¾"	I	H.M.	DB-4-1	DB-4-•	DB-4-7	–		
502A	A	wood	3'-0"	7'-0"	1¾"	I	H.M.	DB-4-1	DB-4-•	DB-4-7	–		
502B	A	wood	3'-0"	7'-0"	1¾"	I	H.M.	DB-4-1	DB-4-•	DB-4-7	–		
204A	A	wood	3'-0"	7'-0"	1¾"	I	H.M.	DB-4-1	DB-4-•	DB-4-7	–		
205A	A	wood	3'-0"	7'-0"	1¾"	I	H.M.	DB-4-3	DB-4-•	DB-4-7	DB-4-•		undercut
206A	A	wood	3'-0"	7'-0"	1¾"	I	H.M.	DB-4-3	DB-4-•	DB-4-7	DB-4-•		undercut
207A													not used
212A													not used

FINISH SCHEDULE KEYS

MATERIAL
A. concrete
B. 1"x 1" mosaic tile
C. carpet
D. 6"x6" quarry tile
E. gypsum board
F. cultured marble
G. 4"x 4" ceramic tile
H. storefront
I. vinyl composition tile
J. resilient base - straight
K. resilient base - cove
L. suspended acoustical ceiling
M. exposed structure

FINISH
1. sealer
2. paint
3. tape and sand
4. factory
5. wax

FINISH SCHEDULE

NO.	NAME	FLOOR MAT.	FLOOR FIN.	BASE MAT.	BASE FIN.	N.WALL MAT.	N.WALL FIN.	E.WALL MAT.	E.WALL FIN.	S.WALL MAT.	S.WALL FIN.	W.WALL MAT.	W.WALL FIN.	CLG. MAT.	CLG. FIN.	REMARKS
101	lease	A	–			E,H	3,4	E	3	E	3	E,H	3,4	L	4	
102	tele./elect.	I	5	K	4	E	2	E	2	E	2	E	2	m	–	
103	corridor	C	4	J	4	E	2	E	2	–	–	E	2	L	4	
104																not used
105	elev. lobby	G	4	J	4	E	2	E	2	E	2	E	2	E	2	
106	elev. equip.	A	1	–	–	E	3	E	3	F	4	E	3	E	3	
107	men	B	4	B	4	E,G	2,4	E,G	2,4	E,G	2,4	E,G	2,4	E	2	
108	women	B	4	B	4	E,G	2,4	E,G	2,4	E,G	2,4	E,G	2,4	E	2	
109	vest.	C	4	J	4	E	2	E	2	–	–	E	2	L	4	
110	lease	A	–	–	–	E,H	3,4	E,H	3,4	E	3	E	3	L	4	
111	corridor	C	4	J	4	E	2	E	2	–	–	L	4			
112	lease	A	–	–	–	E	3	E,H	3,4	E,H	3,4	E	3	L	4	
113	lobby	C	4	J	4	E	2	E	2	H	4	E	2	E	2	
114	vest.	D	4	–	–	E,H	2,4	E,H	2,4	H	4	E,H	2,4	E	2	
115	lease	A	–	–	–	E	3	E	3	E,H	3,4	E,H	3,4	L	4	
116	corridor	C	4	J	4	E	2	–	–	E	2	H	4	L	4	
501	stair 01	A	1	–	–	E	2	E	2	E	2	E	2	m,E	-,2	
502	stair 02	A	1	–	–	E	2	E	2	E	2	E	2	m,E	-,2	
201	lease	A	–	–	–	E,H	3,4	E	3	E	3	E,H	3,4	L	4	
202																not used
203	elev. lobby	C	4	J	4	E	2	E	2	E	2	E	2	E	2	
204	jan.	I	5	K	4	E	3	E	2	E,G	2,4	E,G	2,4	E	3	
205	men	B	4	B	4	E,G	2,4	E,G	2,4	E,G	2,4	E,G	2,4	E	2	
206	women	B	4	B	4	E,G	2,4	E,G	2,4	E,G	2,4	E,G	2,4	E	2	
207	lease	A	–	–	–	E,H	3,4	E	3	E	3	E	3	L	4	
208	vest.	C	4	J	4	E	2	–	–	E	2	E	2	L	4	
209	lease	A	–	–	–	E	3	E,H	3,4	E,H	3,4	E	3	L	4	
210	corridor	C	4	J	4	E	2	E	2	–	–	L	4			
211	corridor	C	4	J	4	E	2	–	–	E	2	E	2	L	4	
212	lease	A	–	–	–	E	3	E	3	E,H	3,4	E,H	3,4	L	4	

The Completed Schedules

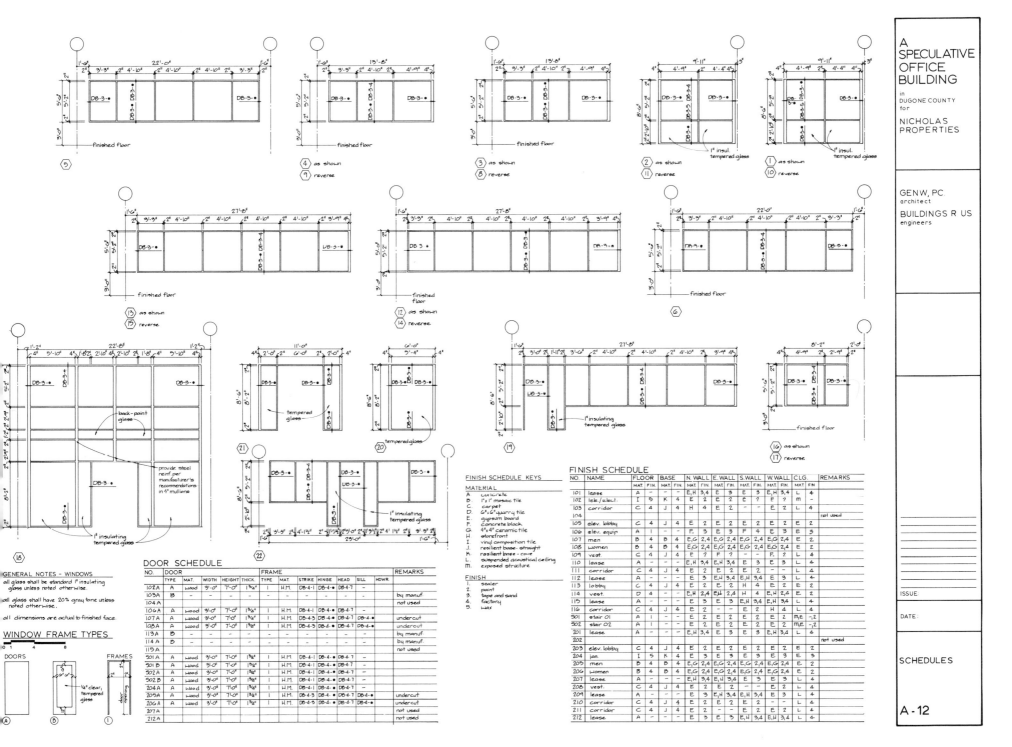

12 Details

Details, along with wall sections, require a more complete knowledge of building assembly than any other construction document. Good detailing can mean the difference between an excellent project and a good project. Many interesting designs have been ruined by sloppy detailing. Thus, a good set of construction documents will include details that have been handled with a thoughtful approach.

■ General Information

The first consideration in detailing is to decide how many details to draft. The number will depend on the complexity of the design, the extent of desired control, the fee, and the contract type. Some clients will hire an architect to do only a "scope" set of construction documents. In these cases, the number of details will be very limited. Many architects also limit the number of details actually drawn with the intent of "picking them up" in the field or during shop drawings; other architects draft virtually every detail, reasoning that the details should be included in the original set of construction documents to ensure their inclusion in the final project. By including virtually every detail, an architect is also assured of complete pricing. It is not unusual for a contractor to tell the field architect that a detail that was not in the original construction documents, but that became necessary or desired at a later date, will incur additional costs. The majority of clients do not like additional costs, particularly when they are not responsible for causing them.

Another reason for extensive detailing at this stage is that details that were intended to be added during shop drawings or actual construction are often overlooked. Although a good field architect can reduce the likelihood of such problems, it is very time-consuming and demanding work. In addition, architects must think about potential liability issues.

Once again, the sample project shown in this book is very basic. Thus, it does not include a great number of special details. Many of the details drafted for this project could be saved in a permanent file for future use and reference. A detail file of typical and standard conditions makes a good reference source for any architect. For example, when you need to draw a curb and gutter for a site plan, it is an easy process to go to the detail file and pull out a reference example. In many cases the existing reference detail will work for a project, while in other cases it may require minor modification. In either case, it will be a great time-saver.

Details may be drafted either directly onto a large sheet or onto 8½- by 11-inch sheets that are numbered and then inserted into a project detail book. There are numerous ways to organize the detail book. One method is to use the CSI (Construction Specifications Institute) format, available from CSI. Another method is to arrange details by usage, which relates more closely to how construction documents are understood. The following eight categories can be used for the grouping of details:

1. *Basic elements.* The basic elements section is a general section where technical aspects of the construction documents can be located. Items included would be:
   a. Title sheet with client name and address and name and address of architect and engineering consultants.
   b. Drawing list giving sheet number and name of every construction document.
   c. Detail book index giving the major categories of details (see page 160).
   d. Material indications reference.
   e. Standard abbreviations used.
   f. Standard symbols used in construction documents.

2. *Site details.*

3. *Building envelope details.* The building envelope is that part of the building that separates the interior from the exterior. It includes the roof, the parapet, the window wall, the curtain wall, and the exterior wall construction.

4. *Partitions.* Walls that divide interior spaces are referred to as partitions. These walls should not be confused with the major walls that divide the interior from the exterior. These exterior walls, which are called wall sections, are included in building envelope details.

5. *Reflected ceiling details.*

6. *Vertical transportation.*

7. *Toilet-room details.*

8. *Miscellaneous details.* Miscellaneous details are those that will not clearly fit into one of the other categories. Attempts should be made to limit the number of these details. (Note: On some projects there may be enough interior architecture to merit a separate category for interior details. In these cases, miscellaneous details would become the ninth category.)

Each detail should include both a category number and a sequence number. These numbers should appear on either the upper or lower right-hand side of the sheet. On pages 161–85, a few details from each category are provided as examples of organization and implementation. There are many more details that could have been selected; areas for which details would typically be drawn are indicated, even if they are not included in the sample set of details. In these instances, the detail includes its standard reference, but ends with a small dark circle instead of a specific number.

DETAIL BOOK INDEX

Concrete Walk with Combination Curb and Gutter
¾″ = 1′-0″ (1 cm = 16 cm)

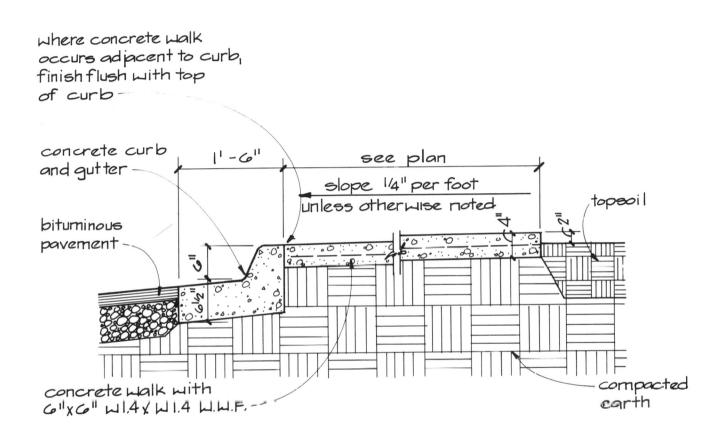

where concrete walk occurs adjacent to curb, finish flush with top of curb

concrete curb and gutter

bituminous pavement

1′-6″

see plan

slope ¼″ per foot unless otherwise noted

topsoil

6″

6½″

4″

2″

concrete walk with 6″×6″ W1.4×W1.4 W.W.F.

compacted earth

Detail 2-2
Concrete Curb and Gutter at Bituminous Paving
1½″ = 1′-0″ (1 cm = 8 cm)

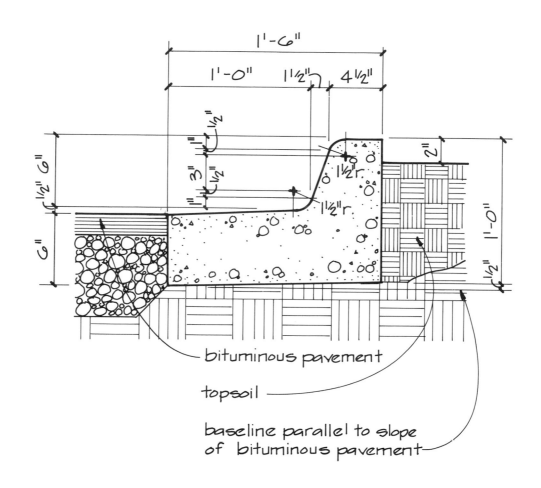

bituminous pavement

topsoil

baseline parallel to slope
of bituminous pavement

Detail 2-3
Brick Bench
3″ = 1′-0″ (1 cm = 4 cm)

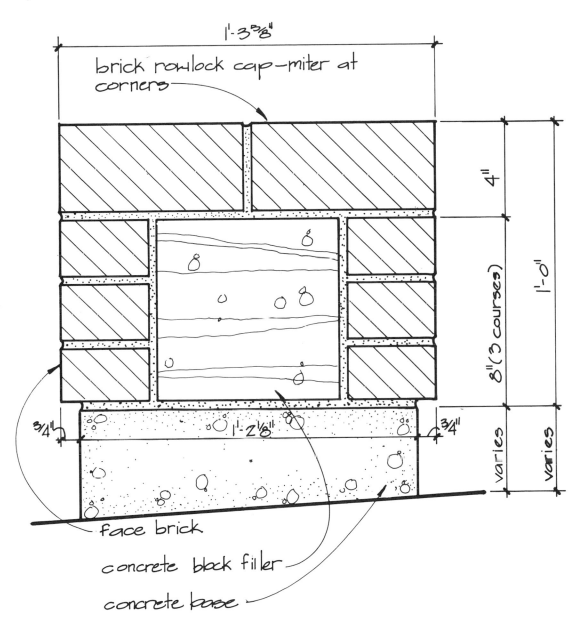

brick rowlock cap-miter at corners

face brick

concrete block filler

concrete base

1′-3⅜″

4″

8″ (3 courses)

1′-0″

¾″

1′-2⅛″

¾″

varies

varies

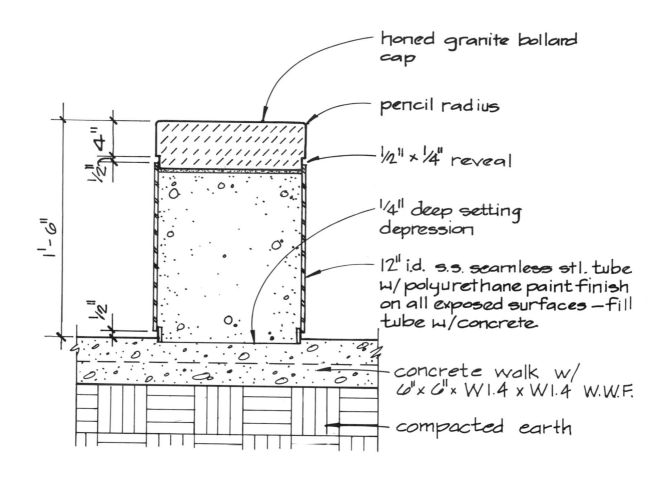

honed granite bollard cap

pencil radius

½" × ¼" reveal

¼" deep setting depression

12" i.d. s.s. seamless stl. tube w/ polyurethane paint finish on all exposed surfaces — fill tube w/concrete

concrete walk w/ 6" × 6" × W1.4 × W1.4 W.W.F.

compacted earth

Detail 3-1
Flashing Detail at Brick and Stud Parapet
3″ = 1′-0″ (1 cm = 4 cm)

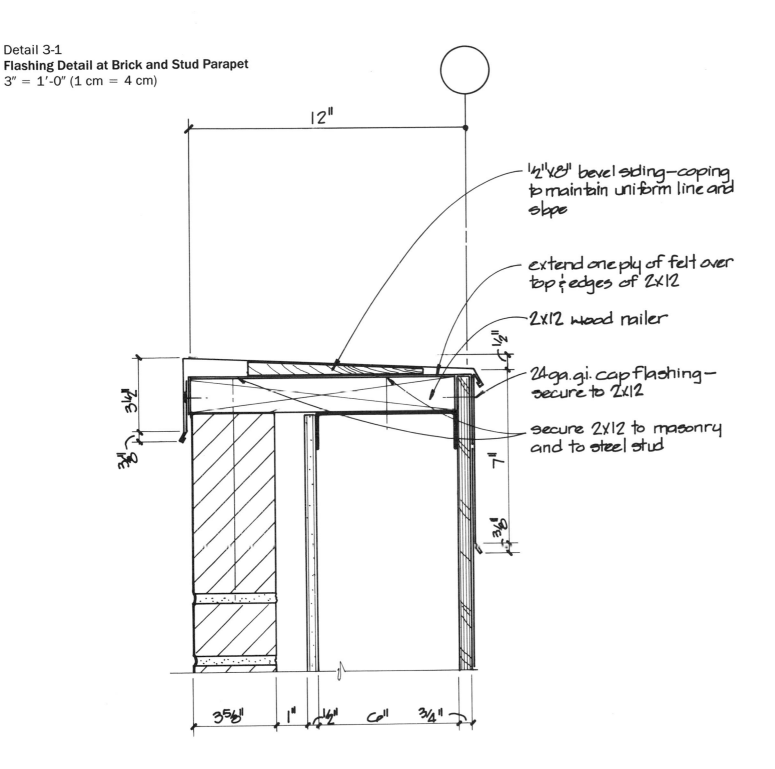

12″

½″x8″ bevel siding—coping to maintain uniform line and slope

extend one ply of felt over top & edges of 2x12

2x12 wood nailer

½″

24 ga. g.i. cap flashing—secure to 2x12

7″

secure 2x12 to masonry and to steel stud

3⅛″

3¾″

3⅜″

3⅝″   1″   ½″   6″   ¾″

Detail 3-2
Roof Drain
1½″ = 1′-0″ (1 cm = 8 cm)

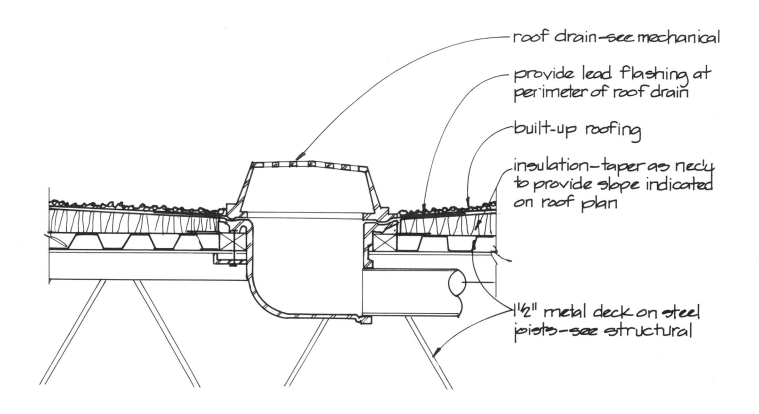

roof drain—see mechanical

provide lead flashing at perimeter of roof drain

built-up roofing

insulation—taper as nec'y to provide slope indicated on roof plan

1½″ metal deck on steel joists—see structural

Detail 3-3
Skylight
¾″ = 1′-0″ (1 cm = 16 cm)

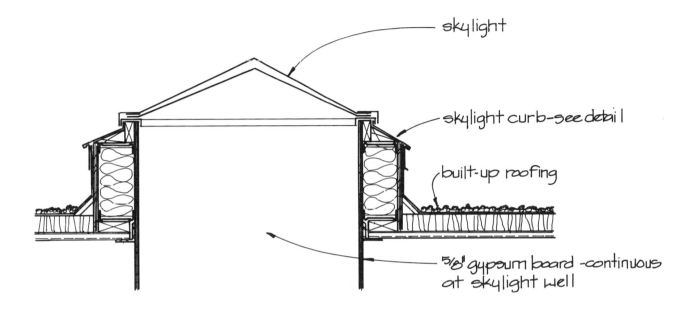

skylight

skylight curb-see detail

built-up roofing

⅝″ gypsum board -continuous at skylight well

Detail 3-4
Head
3″ = 1′-0″ (1 cm = 4 cm)

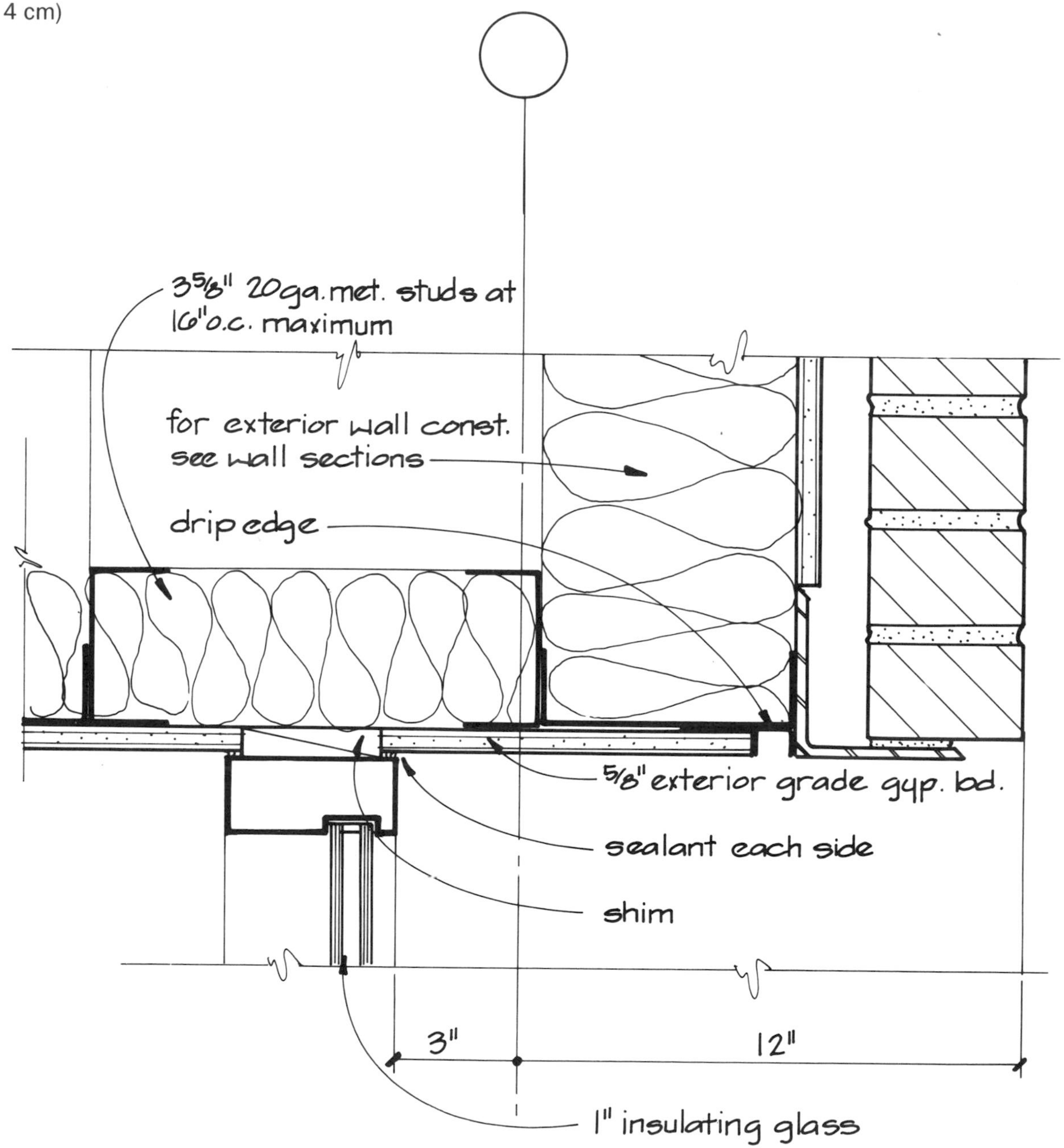

3⅝″ 20 ga. met. studs at 16″ o.c. maximum

for exterior wall const. see wall sections

drip edge

⅝″ exterior grade gyp. bd.

sealant each side

shim

3″

12″

1″ insulating glass

Detail 3-5
Intermediate Horizontal Mullion
3″ = 1′-0″ (1 cm = 4 cm)

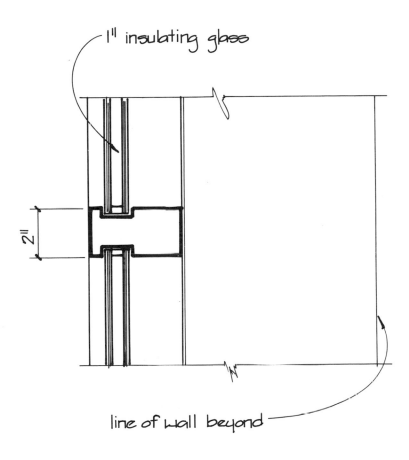

1″ insulating glass

2″

line of wall beyond

Detail 4-1
Fire-Rated Gypsum Board Partition
2″ = 1′-0″ (1 cm = 6 cm)
(Drawing reduced from 3″ = 1′-0″)

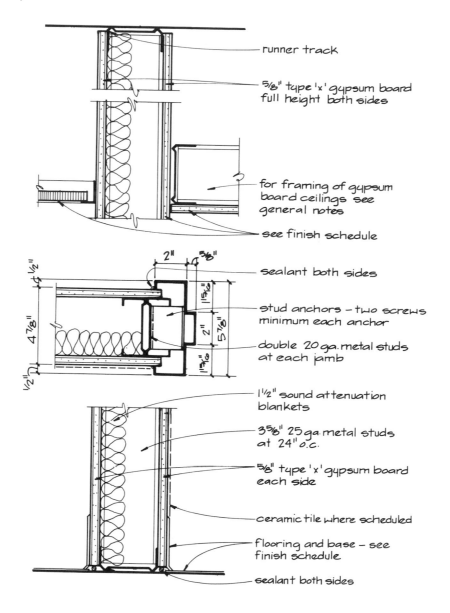

runner track

5/8″ type 'x' gypsum board full height both sides

for framing of gypsum board ceilings see general notes

see finish schedule

sealant both sides

stud anchors – two screws minimum each anchor

double 20 ga. metal studs at each jamb

1 1/2″ sound attenuation blankets

3 5/8″ 25 ga. metal studs at 24″ o.c.

5/8″ type 'x' gypsum board each side

ceramic tile where scheduled

flooring and base – see finish schedule

sealant both sides

Detail 4-2
As Shown (Standard Gypsum Board Partition)

Detail 4-3
**As Shown with Sound Attenuation
and Type "X" Gypsum Board
(Fire-Rated Gypsum Board Partition)**
2" = 1'-0" (1 cm = 6 cm)
(Drawing reduced from 3" = 1'-0")

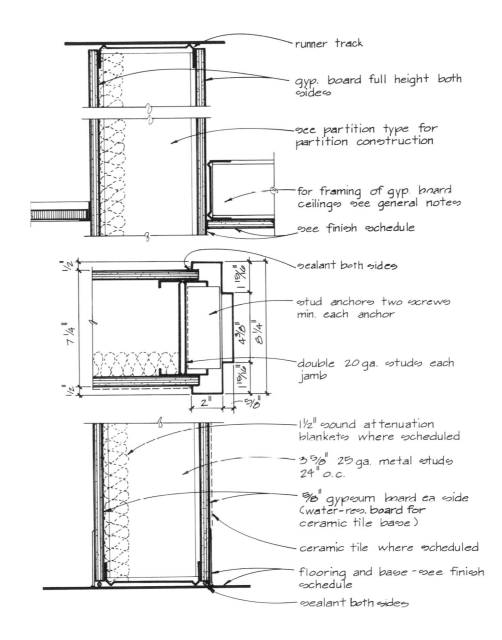

runner track

gyp. board full height both sides

see partition type for partition construction

for framing of gyp. board ceilings see general notes

see finish schedule

sealant both sides

stud anchors two screws min. each anchor

double 20 ga. studs each jamb

1½" sound attenuation blankets where scheduled

3 ⅝" 25 ga. metal studs 24" o.c.

⅝" gypsum board ea. side (water-res. board for ceramic tile base)

ceramic tile where scheduled

flooring and base - see finish schedule

sealant both sides

Detail 4-4
Standard Gypsum Board Chase Wall Partition
2″ = 1'-0″ (1 cm = 6 cm)
(Drawing reduced from 3″ = 1'-0″)

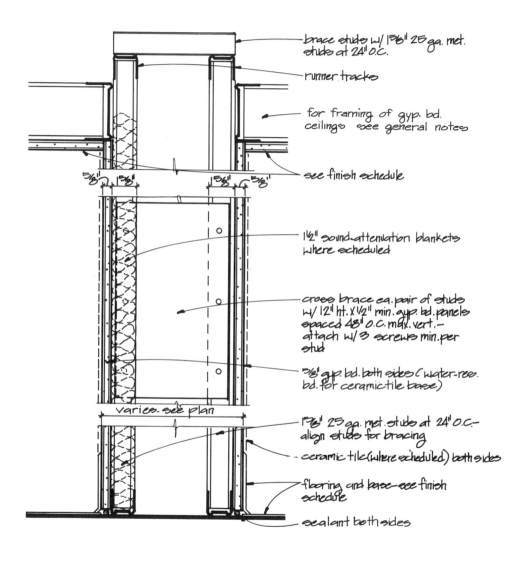

brace studs w/ 1⅝″ 25 ga. met. studs at 24″ o.c.

runner tracks

for framing of gyp. bd. ceilings see general notes

see finish schedule

1½″ sound-attenuation blankets where scheduled

cross brace ea. pair of studs w/ 12″ ht. x ½″ min. gyp. bd. panels spaced 48″ o.c. max. vert.— attach w/ 3 screws min. per stud

⅝″ gyp. bd. both sides (water-res. bd. for ceramic tile base)

1⅝″ 25 ga. met. studs at 24″ o.c.— align studs for bracing

ceramic tile (where scheduled) both sides

flooring and base—see finish schedule

sealant both sides

⅝″ 1⅝″   1⅝″ ⅝″

varies. see plan

Detail 4-5
Standard Gypsum Board Shaft Wall Partition
2″ = 1′-0″ (1 cm = 6 cm)
(Drawing reduced from 3″ = 1′-0″)

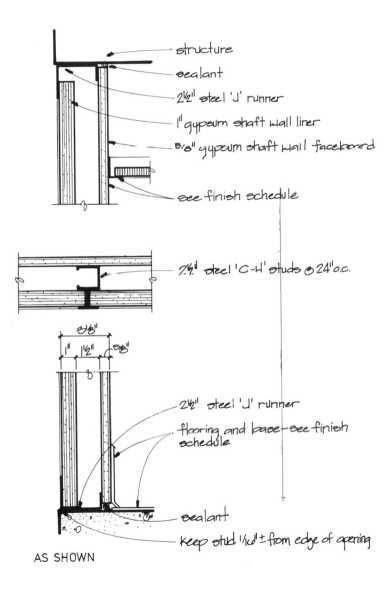

structure

sealant

2½″ steel 'J' runner

1″ gypsum shaft wall liner

⅝″ gypsum shaft wall faceboard

see finish schedule

2½″ steel 'C-H' studs @ 24″ o.c.

2½″ steel 'J' runner

flooring and base–see finish schedule

sealant

keep stud ¹⁄₁₆″ ± from edge of opening

AS SHOWN

173

Detail 4-6
Masonry Partition—Furred 8″ Concrete Block
2″ = 1′-0″ (1 cm = 6 cm)
(Drawing reduced from 3″ = 1′-0″)

DETAIL 13

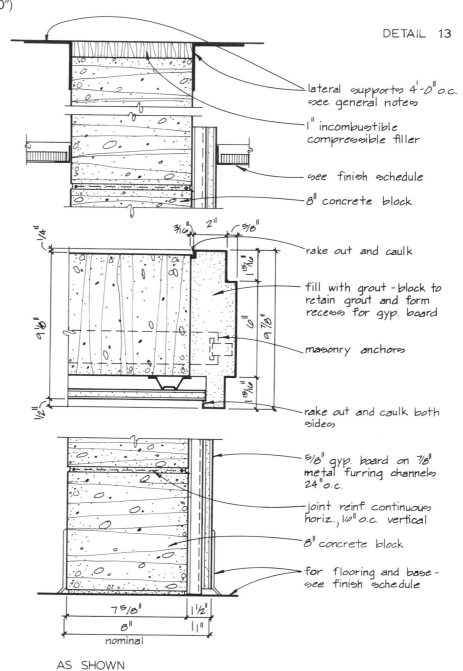

lateral supports 4′-0″ o.c.
see general notes

1″ incombustible compressible filler

see finish schedule

8″ concrete block

rake out and caulk

fill with grout - block to retain grout and form recess for gyp. board

masonry anchors

rake out and caulk both sides

5/8″ gyp. board on 7/8″ metal furring channels 24″ o.c.

joint reinf continuous horiz., 16″ o.c. vertical

8″ concrete block

for flooring and base - see finish schedule

AS SHOWN

174

Detail 4-7
Door Head
3″ = 1′-0″ (1 cm = 4 cm)

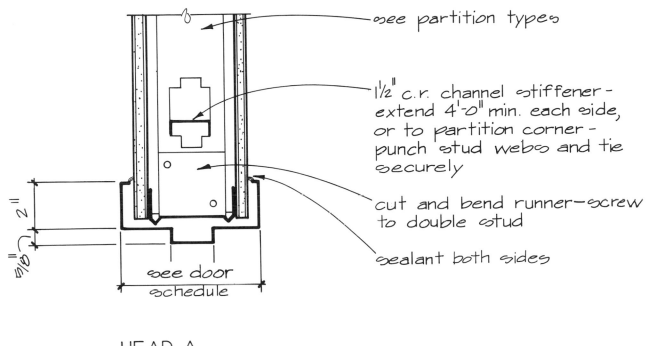

see partition types

1½″ c.r. channel stiffener -
extend 4′-0″ min. each side,
or to partition corner -
punch stud webs and tie
securely

cut and bend runner—screw
to double stud

sealant both sides

see door
schedule

2″

5/8″

HEAD A

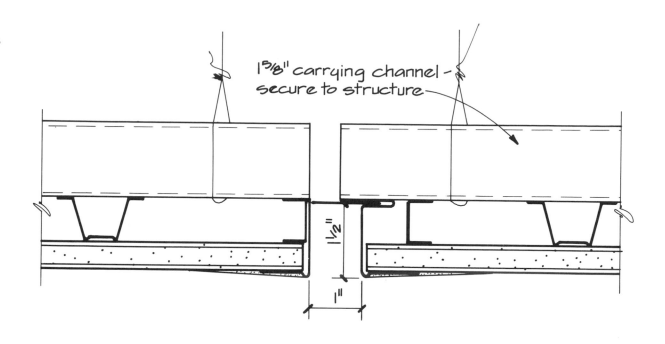

1⅝" carrying channel – secure to structure

1½"

1"

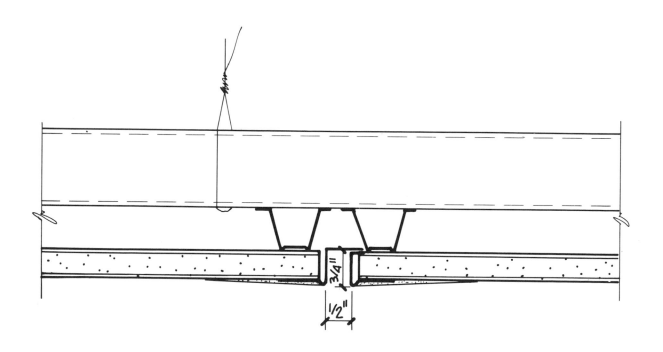

¾"

½"

Detail 5-2
Concealed Light in Soffit with Louver
1½" = 1'-0" (1 cm = 8 cm)

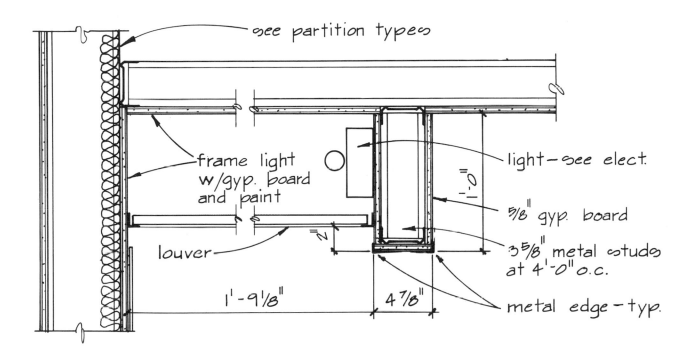

see partition types

frame light
w/gyp. board
and paint

louver

light—see elect.

⅝" gyp. board

3⅝" metal studs
at 4'-0" o.c.

metal edge—typ.

1'-9⅛"

4⅞"

1'-0"

2"

Detail 5-3
Ceiling Level Change
$1\frac{1}{2}'' = 1'\text{-}0''$ (1 cm = 8 cm)

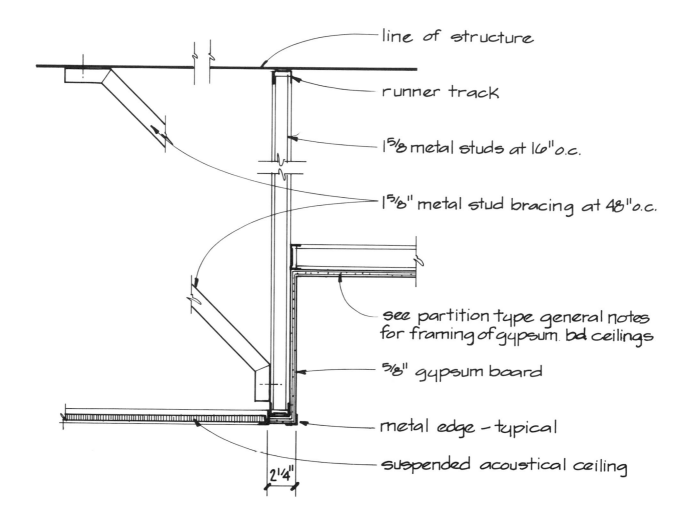

line of structure

runner track

$1\frac{5}{8}$ metal studs at 16" o.c.

$1\frac{5}{8}''$ metal stud bracing at 48" o.c.

see partition type general notes for framing of gypsum. bd ceilings

$\frac{5}{8}''$ gypsum board

metal edge - typical

suspended acoustical ceiling

$2\frac{1}{4}''$

Detail 6-1
Intermediate Stair Landing
¾″ = 1′-0″ (1 cm = 16 cm)
(Drawing reduced from 1″ = 1′-0″)

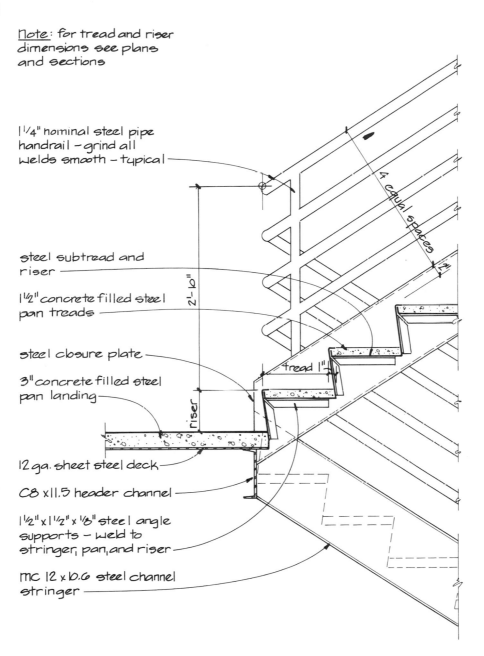

Note: for tread and riser dimensions see plans and sections

1¼" nominal steel pipe handrail – grind all welds smooth – typical

steel subtread and riser

1½" concrete filled steel pan treads

steel closure plate

3" concrete filled steel pan landing

12 ga. sheet steel deck

C8 x 11.5 header channel

1½" x 1½" x ⅛" steel angle supports – weld to stringer, pan, and riser

MC 12 x 10.6 steel channel stringer

4 equal spaces

2′-10″

riser

tread 1″

Detail 6-2
Stair Landing
1″ = 1′-0″ (1 cm = 12 cm)

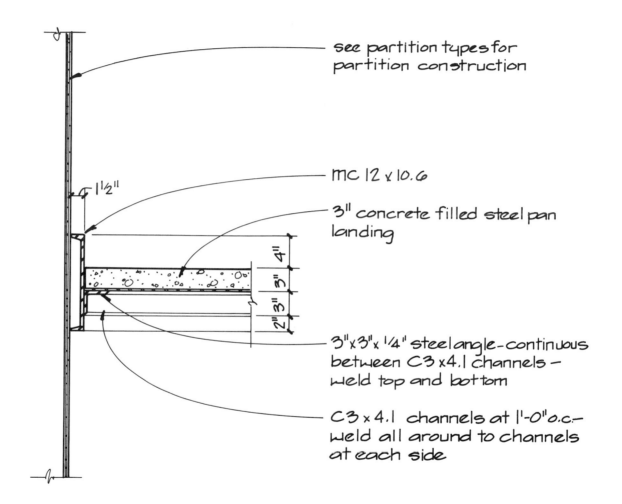

see partition types for
partition construction

mc 12 x 10.6

3″ concrete filled steel pan
landing

1½″

2″ 3″ 3″ 4″

3″ x 3″ x ¼″ steel angle - continuous
between C3 x 4.1 channels -
weld top and bottom

C3 x 4.1 channels at 1′-0″ o.c.-
weld all around to channels
at each side

Detail 6-3
Wall-Handrail Detail
¾" = 1'-0" (1 cm = 16 cm)
(Drawing reduced from 1" = 1'-0")

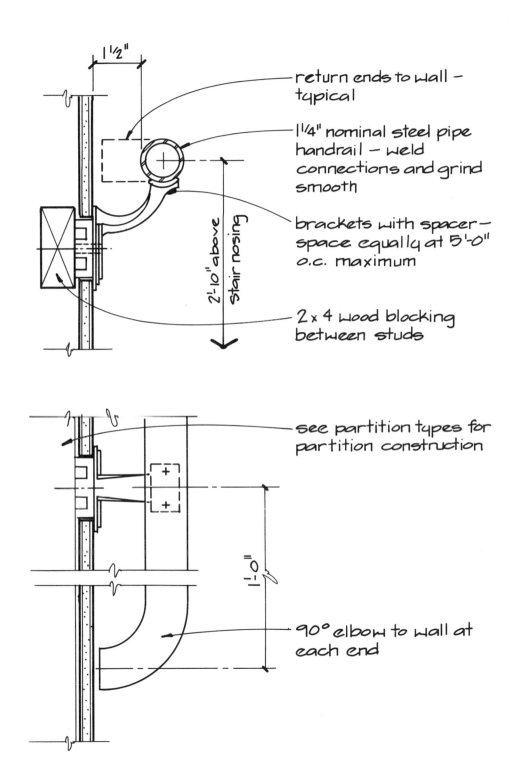

1½"

return ends to wall – typical

1¼" nominal steel pipe handrail – weld connections and grind smooth

brackets with spacer – space equally at 5'-0" o.c. maximum

2 x 4 wood blocking between studs

2'-10" above stair nosing

see partition types for partition construction

1'-0"

90° elbow to wall at each end

Detail 6-4
Head at Elevator
3″ = 1′-0″ (1 cm = 4 cm)

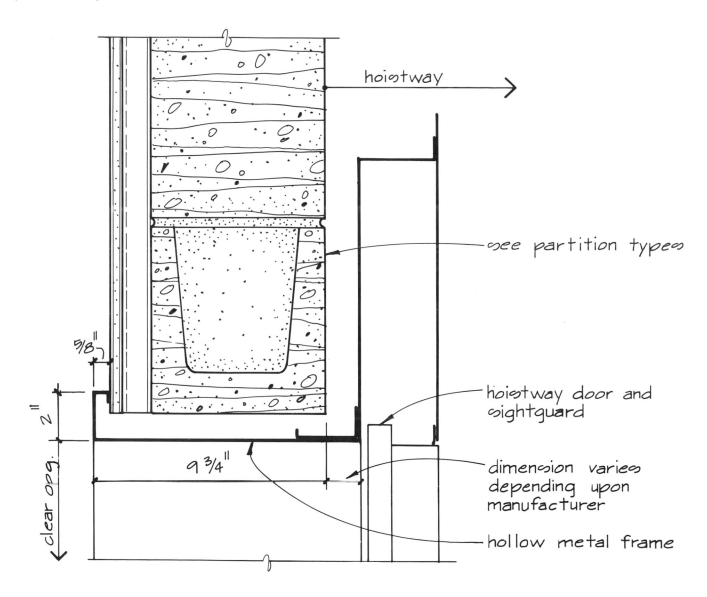

hoistway

see partition types

5/8″

2″

clear opg.

9 3/4″

hoistway door and sightguard

dimension varies depending upon manufacturer

hollow metal frame

Detail 6-5
Jamb at Elevator
3″ = 1′-0″ (1 cm = 4 cm)

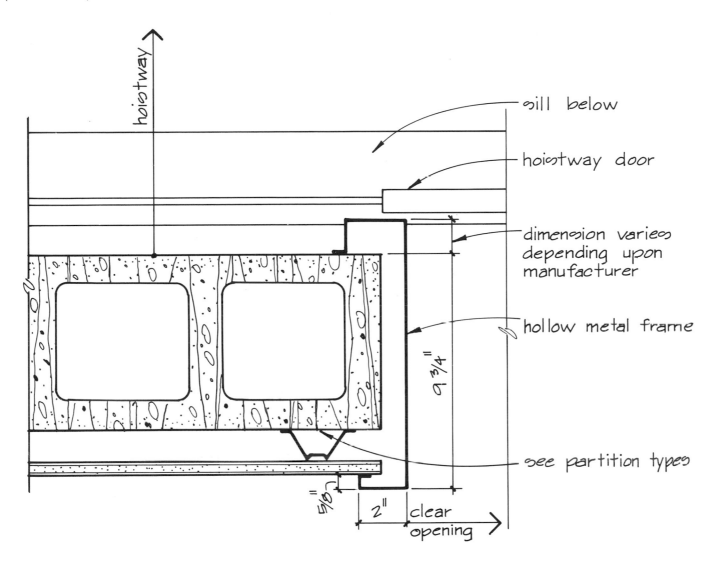

hoistway

sill below

hoistway door

dimension varies depending upon manufacturer

hollow metal frame

9 3/4″

see partition types

5/8″

2″

clear opening

Detail 7-1
Lavatory Countertop with Reveal
3″ = 1′-0″ (1 cm = 4 cm)

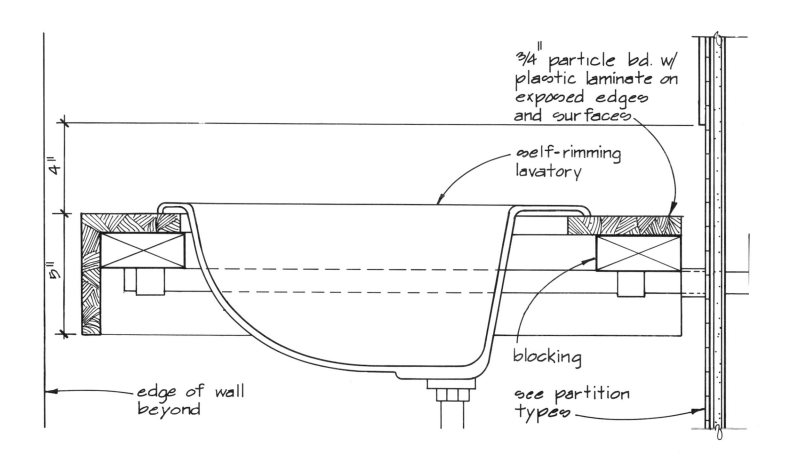

3/4″ particle bd. w/ plastic laminate on exposed edges and surfaces

self-rimming lavatory

4″

5″

edge of wall beyond

blocking

see partition types

Detail 7-2
Grab Bar—Detail
3″ = 1′-0″ (1 cm = 4 cm)

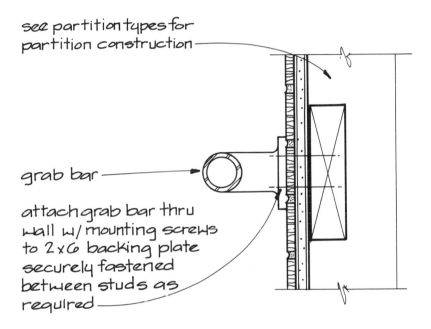

see partition types for
partition construction

grab bar

attach grab bar thru
wall w/ mounting screws
to 2 x 6 backing plate
securely fastened
between studs as
required

Appendix

■ APPENDIX A: MISCELLANEOUS FORMS AND DRAWING AIDS

Included in this appendix are;
1. Material Indications
2. Standard Abbreviations
3. Door Schedule (Blank)
4. Finish Schedule (Blank)
5. Lettering Guide

	asphalt or bituminous paving
	batt insulation
	brick
	concrete
	concrete block
	earth
	gravel
	gypsum board or sheathing
	metal stud partition
	particle board
	plywood
	precast concrete
	rigid insulation
	steel
	topsoil
	wood

STANDARD ABBREVIATIONS

a.f.f.	above finished floor	**col.**	column	**f.d.**	floor drain
a.f.g.	above finished grade	**conc.**	concrete	**f.h.**	flat head
acous.	acoustical	**const.**	construction	**fdn.**	foundation
adj.	adjustable	**cont.**	continuous	**fin.**	finish
alum.	aluminum	**dbl.**	double	**flr.**	floor
anch.	anchor	**det.**	detail	**fluor.**	fluorescent
approx.	approximately	**dia., ϕ**	diameter	**frm.**	frame
asb.	asbestos	**diag.**	diagonal	**ft.**	foot
atten.	attenuation	**dim.**	dimension	**ftg.**	footing
bd.	board	**disp.**	dispenser	**g.i.**	galvanized iron
bldg.	building	**dn.**	down	**ga.**	gauge
blk.	block	**dwg.**	drawing	**galv.**	galvanized
bm.	beam	**e.j.**	expansion joint	**gen.**	general
bot.	bottom	**e.w.c.**	electric water cooler	**gl.**	glass
c.b.	catch basin	**ea.**	each	**grt.**	grout
c.g.	corner guard	**el.**	elevation	**gyp.**	gypsum
c.j.	control joint	**elect.**	electrical	**gyp. bd.**	gypsum board
c.m.u.	concrete masonry unit	**enam.**	enamel	**h.m.**	hollow metal
c.o.	clean out	**eq.**	equal	**h.r.**	handrail
c.r.	cold rolled	**equip.**	equipment	**hd.**	head
cab.	cabinet	**exist.**	existing	**hdwd.**	hardwood
cem.	cement	**exp.**	expansion	**horiz.**	horizontal
cer.	ceramic	**exp. jt.**	expansion joint	**ht.**	height
clg.	ceiling	**ext.**	exterior	**i.d.**	inside diameter

in.	inch	**plas.**	plaster	**std.**	standard
insul.	insulation	**plwd.**	plywood	**stl.**	steel
int.	interior	**porc.**	porcelain	**struct.**	structural
inv.	invert	**q.t.**	quarry tile	**susp.**	suspended
j.b.	junction box	**r.**	risers	**t.**	treads
jt.	joint	**r.d.**	roof drain	**t. & b.**	top and bottom
lam.	laminate	**r.o.**	rough opening	**t. & g.**	tongue and groove
lav.	lavatory	**rad.**	radius	**t.o.c.**	top of concrete
lt.wt.	lightweight	**re**	reference	**tel.**	telephone
m.h.	manhole	**rec.**	recessed	**thru**	through
m.o.	masonry opening	**reinf.**	reinforced	**typ.**	typical
mach.	machine	**req'd**	required	**ur.**	urinal
manuf.	manufacturer	**res.**	resistant	**v.c.p.**	vitrified clay pipe
max.	maximum	**resil.**	resilient	**v.c.t.**	vinyl composition tile
mech.	mechanical	**ret.**	retaining	**vert.**	vertical
met.	metal	**rm.**	room	**w/**	with
min.	minimum	**s.s.**	stainless steel	**w.c.**	water closet
nec'y	necessary	**s.v.**	sheet vinyl	**w.f.**	wide flange
nom.	nominal	**sched.**	schedule	**w.p.**	waterproof
o.c.	on center	**sect.**	section	**w.w.f.**	welded wire fabric
o.d.	outside diameter	**sht.**	sheet	**water-res.**	water-resistant
opg.	opening	**sim.**	similar	**wd.**	wood
partn.	partition	**spec.**	specification		
pl.	plate	**sq.**	square		

DOOR SCHEDULE

NO.	DOOR					FRAME							REMARKS
	TYPE	MAT.	WIDTH	HEIGHT	THICK.	TYPE	MAT.	STRIKE	HINGE	HEAD	SILL	HDWR.	

FINISH SCHEDULE

NO.	NAME	FLOOR		BASE		N. WALL		E. WALL		S. WALL		W. WALL		CLG.		REMARKS
		MAT.	FIN.	MAT.	FIN.	MAT.	FIN.	MAT.	FIN.	MAT.	FIN.	MAT.	FIN.	MAT.	FIN.	

Using a checklist helps ensure that nothing has been overlooked in the process of preparing a set of construction documents. When you feel that you have finished a set of documents in its entirety, you should use the following checklists to verify that all of the information that is necessary for each drawing has been included on the final document. More extensive checklists are available from other sources; however, by following the enclosed checklists, you will be assured of having included all of the information necessary for a general set of construction documents.

Over a period of time you should develop your own checklists. By adding to the lists here you will already have a good start on this process. Your expanded checklists will make the system more personalized and complete from your individual point of view.

In preparing construction documents, you should always keep in mind the importance of the work. There is usually a tremendous amount of money at stake. Lives are also at stake. Although no one is expected to never make a mistake, you should try hard to minimize the number of errors in your work. A good way to do this is to always check your work.

TITLE BLOCK AND DRAWING INDEX CHECKLIST

☐ Project name
☐ Project location
☐ Client name
☐ Architect's name
☐ Consultant names
☐ Issue block
☐ Architect's seal
☐ Date
☐ Sheet title
☐ Sheet number

SITE PLANS CHECKLIST

As noted in Chapter 2, the site plan is actually composed of three separate plans. In order to simplify this checklist, however, the information included is largely relevant to the architectural site plan.

- ☐ Title block information (sheet title and number)
- ☐ Drawing titles and scales
- ☐ North arrow (incorporated into drawing title)
- ☐ Property line
- ☐ Note referencing name of site surveyor
- ☐ Note to include the soils report as a part of the documents
- ☐ Heavy outline of building footprint with finished floor elevation labeled
- ☐ Street names for adjoining streets
- ☐ Utility lines, powerpoles, transformers, traffic signals, manholes
- ☐ All exterior lighting including references to detail book
- ☐ Concrete walks with expansion joints labeled and referenced to detail book
- ☐ Building located dimensionally from a property line
- ☐ Parking area located dimensionally
- ☐ Radius information dimensioned and noted
- ☐ Handicap parking spaces designated
- ☐ Benchmark location and elevation
- ☐ Existing grades
- ☐ New grades
- ☐ Existing spot elevations
- ☐ New spot elevations
- ☐ Fire hydrants
- ☐ Existing trees and shrubs to remain
- ☐ Test holes from soils testing indicated
- ☐ Drive details referenced to detail book
- ☐ Sign details referenced to detail book
- ☐ Gutter details referenced to detail book
- ☐ Curb details referenced to detail book
- ☐ Handicap ramp details/plans referenced to detail book
- ☐ Other miscellaneous details referenced to detail book
- ☐ Material indications

FLOOR PLANS CHECKLIST

- ☐ Title block information (sheet title and number)
- ☐ Drawing titles and scales
- ☐ North arrow (incorporated into drawing title)
- ☐ Site features immediately adjacent to building
- ☐ Finished floor elevation indicated with a bullet
- ☐ Column centerlines extending through the entire plan
- ☐ Column designation bubbles labeled
- ☐ General note about dimension system that is being used
- ☐ Structural bays dimensioned
- ☐ Overall building length and width dimensioned
- ☐ All changes in planes on exterior walls dimensioned
- ☐ All penetrations in exterior walls dimensioned (i.e., windows and doors)
- ☐ Interior partitions dimensioned (including partition thicknesses) by continuous strings
- ☐ All penetrations in interior walls dimensioned (i.e., door openings)
- ☐ Plumbing fixture locations dimensioned (unless there will be an enlarged plan drawn)
- ☐ Shafts clearly indicated and dimensioned
- ☐ Miscellaneous interior features dimensioned (only those that do not occur on enlarged plans)
- ☐ Partition types indicated and referenced to detail book

- ☐ Wall sections cross-referenced
- ☐ Building sections cross-referenced
- ☐ Enlarged plans cross-referenced
- ☐ Interior elevations cross-referenced
- ☐ Building elevations cross-referenced
- ☐ Door types
- ☐ Room names and numbers
- ☐ Transformers, panel boxes, and telephone boards located and referenced to the appropriate engineering discipline
- ☐ Roof drain leaders drawn and referenced to the appropriate discipline
- ☐ Floor drains drawn and referenced to the appropriate discipline
- ☐ HVAC equipment referenced to the appropriate discipline
- ☐ Structure drawn and referenced to the structural consultant
- ☐ Casework and countertops referenced to detail book
- ☐ Directional arrows on stair plans (even if an enlarged plan is drawn)
- ☐ Recessed door mats dimensioned and referenced to detail book
- ☐ Material indications

ROOF PLANS CHECKLIST

☐ Title block information (sheet title and number)
☐ Drawing titles and scales
☐ North arrow (incorporated into drawing title)
☐ Roof slope elevations labeled with spot elevations
☐ Column centerlines not extending through the entire plan
☐ Column designation bubbles labeled
☐ General note about dimensioning system that is being used
☐ Structural bays dimensioned
☐ Overall building length and width dimensioned
☐ Major features of roof dimensioned
   (including rooftop mechanical equipment)
☐ Roof drains dimensioned and referenced to the
   appropriate discipline and to the detail book
☐ Wall sections cross-referenced
☐ Building sections cross-referenced
☐ HVAC equipment referenced to the appropriate discipline
☐ Parapet details referenced to detail book
☐ Roof hatches referenced to detail book
☐ Skylights referenced to detail book
☐ Roof curbs referenced to detail book
☐ Other miscellaneous details referenced to detail book
☐ Material indications

REFLECTED CEILING PLANS CHECKLIST

☐ Title block information (sheet title and number)
☐ Drawing titles and scales
☐ North arrow (incorporated into drawing title)
☐ Ceiling heights indicated
☐ Column centerlines not drawn through entire plan
☐ Column designation bubbles labeled
☐ General note about dimensioning system that is being used
☐ Structural bays dimensioned
☐ Overall building length and width dimensioned
☐ Interior partitions that do not penetrate the ceiling plane
    drawn as double lines with no pattern
☐ Interior partitions that do penetrate the ceiling plane
    drawn as a double line with a dashed pattern on the inner line
☐ All penetrations in interior partitions
    that occur above the ceiling plane dimensioned
☐ Metal access panels provided for access
    into areas above gypsum board ceilings
☐ Metal access panel locations dimensioned
☐ Lighting fixture locations dimensioned where necessary
☐ Sprinkler head locations dimensioned where necessary
☐ Air device locations dimensioned where necessary
☐ Doors into rooms drawn lightly
☐ Control joints in gypsum board ceilings
    labeled and referenced to detail book
☐ Skylight details referenced to detail book
☐ Soffit details referenced to detail book
☐ Ceilings that are open to structure above appropriately noted
☐ Other miscellaneous details referenced to detail book
☐ Material indications

EXTERIOR ELEVATIONS CHECKLIST

☐ Title block information (sheet title and number)
☐ Drawing titles and scales
☐ Finished floor elevations indicated with a bullet
☐ Column centerlines not extending through the entire elevation
☐ Column designation bubbles labeled
☐ General note about dimension system that is being used
☐ Finished grade at building face drawn as heavy line
☐ Elevation of exterior features indicated with an elevation bullet
☐ Wall sections cross-referenced
☐ Building sections cross-referenced
☐ Control joints labeled and referenced to detail book
☐ Window types indicated
☐ Sign details referenced to detail book
☐ Roof scuppers noted
☐ Building-mounted lighting fixtures noted and
  referenced to the appropriate discipline
☐ Building-mounted mechanical devices noted,
  referenced to the appropriate discipline,
  and referenced to the detail book as necessary
☐ Building-mounted plumbing features noted
  and referenced to the appropriate discipline
☐ Roof materials indicated (for pitched roofs)
☐ Roof slopes noted (for pitched roofs)
☐ Special finishing details noted
☐ Other miscellaneous details referenced to detail book
☐ Material indications

BUILDING SECTIONS CHECKLIST

☐ Title block information (sheet title and number)
☐ Drawing titles and scales
☐ Finished floor elevations indicated with a bullet
☐ Column centerlines extending through the entire section
☐ Column designation bubbles labeled
☐ General note about dimension system that is being used
☐ Roof slopes correctly drawn
☐ Other building sections cross-referenced
☐ Room names and numbers
☐ Structural foundations, footings, and/or
  caissons drawn as broken lines if beyond
☐ Other miscellaneous details referenced to detail book
☐ Material indications

WALL SECTIONS CHECKLIST

☐ Title block information (sheet title and number)
☐ Drawing titles and scales
☐ Finished floor elevations indicated with a bullet
☐ Column centerlines extending
   through the entire wall section
☐ Column designation bubbles labeled
☐ General note about dimension system that is being used
☐ Roof slopes drawn correctly
☐ Structural foundations, footings, and/or
   caissons drawn as broken lines if beyond
☐ Other miscellaneous details referenced to detail book
☐ Material indications

VERTICAL TRANSPORTATION CHECKLIST

☐ Title block information (sheet title and number)
☐ Drawing titles and scales
☐ Plans—north arrow (incorporated into drawing title)
☐ Finished floor elevations indicated with a bullet
☐ Column centerlines extending through the entire drawing
☐ Column designation bubbles labeled
☐ General note about dimension system that is being used
☐ Plans—door types
☐ Plans—room names and numbers
☐ Ladder details referenced to detail book
☐ Stairs—handrail details referenced to detail book
☐ Stairs—guardrail details referenced to detail book
☐ Plans—partition types indicated and
   referenced to detail book
☐ Sections cross-referenced from plans
☐ Structural features noted and referenced
   to the structural consultant as appropriate
☐ Interior partitions dimensioned (including
   partition thicknesses) by continuous strings
☐ All penetrations in interior walls dimensioned
   (i.e., door openings)
☐ Stairs/Plans—directional arrows
☐ Other miscellaneous details referenced to detail book
☐ Material indications

ENLARGED PLANS AND INTERIOR ELEVATIONS CHECKLIST

- [ ] Title block information (sheet title and number)
- [ ] Drawing titles and scales
- [ ] North arrow on plans (incorporated into drawing title)
- [ ] Plans—finished floor elevations indicated with a bullet
- [ ] Plans—column centerlines extending through the entire drawing
- [ ] Plans—column designation bubbles labeled
- [ ] General note about dimension system that is being used
- [ ] Interior partitions dimensioned (including partition thicknesses) by continuous strings
- [ ] All penetrations in interior walls dimensioned (i.e., doors)
- [ ] Plumbing fixture locations dimensioned
- [ ] Shafts clearly indicated and dimensioned
- [ ] Plans—partition types indicated and referenced to detail book
- [ ] Plans—wall sections cross-referenced as necessary
- [ ] Interior elevations referenced
- [ ] Plans—door types
- [ ] Plans—room names and numbers
- [ ] Floor drains drawn and referenced to the appropriate discipline
- [ ] HVAC equipment referenced to the appropriate discipline
- [ ] Structure drawn and referenced to the structural consultant
- [ ] Casework and countertops referenced to detail book
- [ ] Other miscellaneous details referenced to detail book
- [ ] Material indications

SCHEDULES CHECKLIST

☐ Title block information
  (sheet title and number)
☐ Drawing titles and scales
☐ Windows—general note about
  dimension system that is being used
☐ Windows—column centerlines
☐ Windows—column designation bubbles labeled
☐ Windows—detail cuts referenced to detail book

Included in this appendix are all of the final construction
documents that have been used in the body of the book.

SEQUENCING OF DRAWINGS

Drawing Number/Name	Phase I	Phase II	Phase III	Phase IV
A-1 Site Plan	████	████	████	
A-2 Floor Plans	████	████	████	████
A-3 Roof Plan	████	████	████	
A-4 Reflected Ceiling Plans		████	████	████
A-5 Exterior Elevations	████	████	████	
A-6 Building Sections			████	
A-7 Wall Sections		████	████	████
A-8 Vertical Transportation		████	████	████
A-9 Enlarged Plans and Interior Elevations		████	████	
A-10 Schedules			████	████

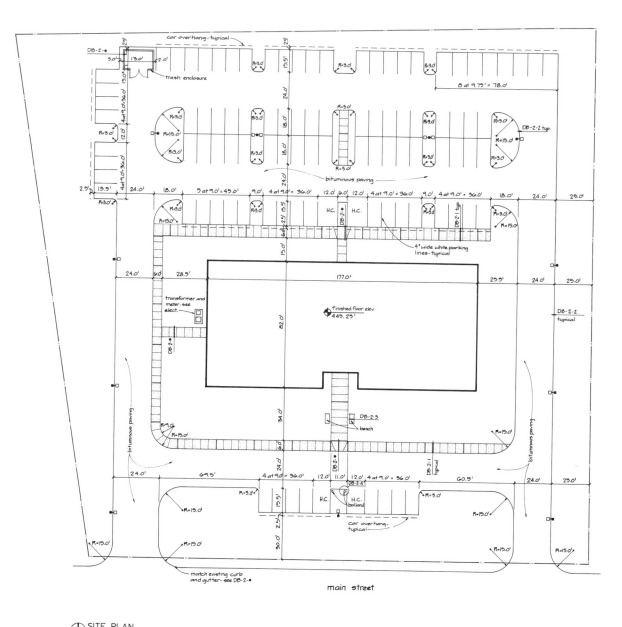

car overhang - typical

DB-2-•
3.0' 13.0' 2.0'

trash enclosure

8 at 9.75' = 78.0'

R=3.0' 15.5' 2.5'

R=3.0' R=3.0'

24.0'

R=3.0' 18.0' R=3.0' DB-2-2 typ.

R=15.0' 18.0' R=3.0'

R=3.0' 24.0' bituminous paving

R=3.0'

2.5' 15.5' 24.0' 18.0' 5 at 9.0'= 45.0' 9.0' 4 at 9.0'=36.0' 12.0' 6.0' 12.0' 4 at 9.0'= 36.0' 9.0' 4 at 9.0'= 36.0' 18.0' 24.0' 25.0'

R=3.0' R=3.0' R=3.0' H.C. H.C. R=3.0' DB-2-1 typ. R=3.0'

R=15.0' 15.0' DB-2- R=15.0'

4" wide white parking
lines - typical

24.0' 6.0' 28.5' 177.0' 25.5' 24.0' 25.0'

transformer and
meter - see
elect.

finished floor elev.
445.25'

82.0' DB-2-

DB-2-2
typical

bituminous paving bituminous paving

34.0' DB-2-3

bench

R=9.0' R=15.0'

R=15.0'

24.0' 69.5' 4 at 9.0' = 36.0' 12.0' 11.0' 4 at 9.0' = 36.0' 60.5' 24.0' 25.0'

R=9.0' 15.5' H.C. DB-2-4 R=9.0' R=15.0'

H.C.
bollard

30.0' 2.5' car overhang -
typical

R=15.0' R=15.0' R=15.0' R=15.0'

match existing curb
and gutter - see DB-2-•

main street

SITE PLAN
0 5 20 40

GENERAL NOTES AND SYMBOLS
all dimensions are actual to finished face

for landscaping features see landscape plan

for site grading, utilities, and elevation see civil

H.C. - handicap parking - stencil handicap symbol
onto bituminous paving with white paint

•-□ site lighting - see electrical

expansion joint - see DB-2-•

A
SPECULATIVE
OFFICE
BUILDING
in
DUGONE COUNTY
for

NICHOLAS
PROPERTIES

GENW, PC.
architect

BUILDINGS R US
engineers

ISSUE:

DATE:

SITE PLAN

A-1

208

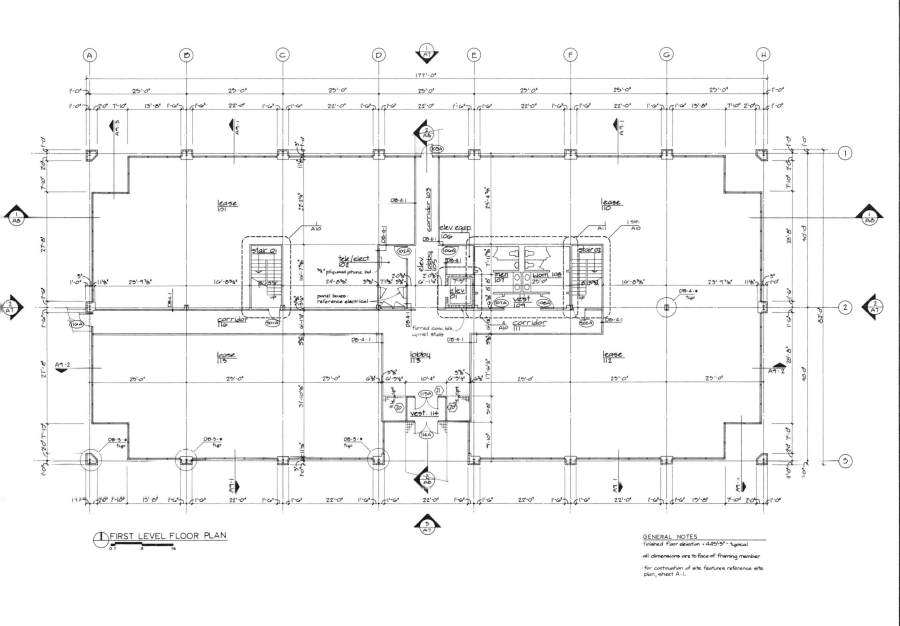

① FIRST LEVEL FLOOR PLAN

GENERAL NOTES

· finished floor elevation · 445'-5" · typical

· all dimensions are to face of framing member

· for continuation of site features reference site plan, sheet A-1.

A
SPECULATIVE
OFFICE
BUILDING

in
DUGONE COUNTY
for

NICHOLAS
PROPERTIES

GEN W, PC.
architect

BUILDINGS R US
engineers

ISSUE:

DATE:

FIRST LEVEL
FLOOR PLAN

A-2

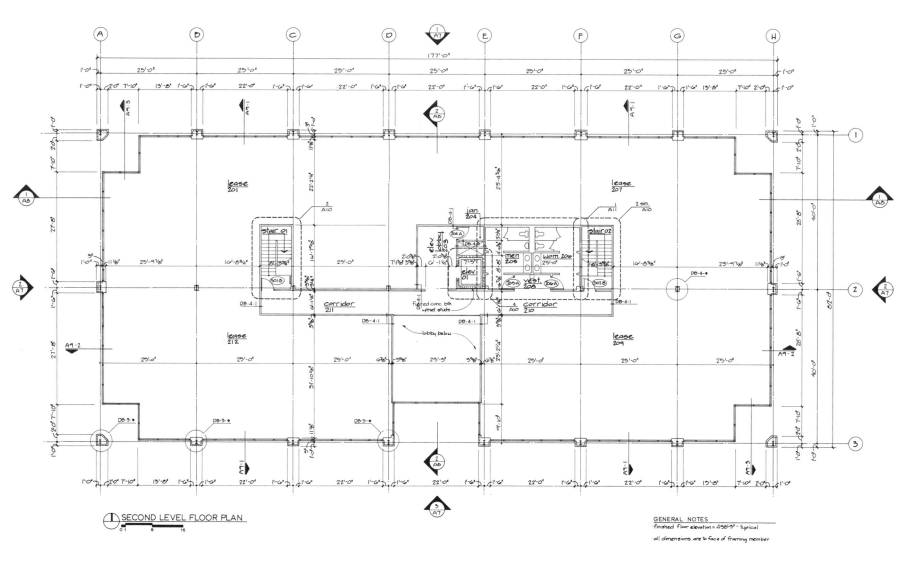

A
SPECULATIVE
OFFICE
BUILDING
in
DUGONE COUNTY
for

NICHOLAS
PROPERTIES

GENW, PC
architect

BUILDINGS R US
engineers

ISSUE:

DATE:

SECOND LEVEL
FLOOR PLAN

A-3

SECOND LEVEL FLOOR PLAN

lease
201

lease
207

lease
212

lease
209

stair 01

stair 02

jan.
204

elev.
lobby
203

men
205

wom. 206

corridor
211

corridor
210

vest.
208

elev.
01

lobby below

GENERAL NOTES
·finished floor elevation = 456'-3" - typical

·all dimensions are to face of framing member

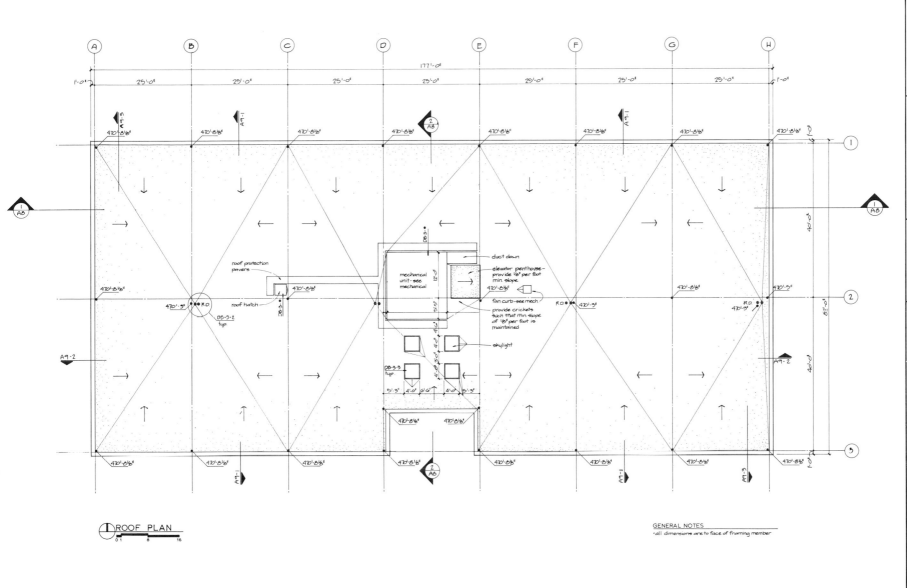

ROOF PLAN

A
SPECULATIVE
OFFICE
BUILDING
in
DUGONE COUNTY
for

NICHOLAS
PROPERTIES

GEN W, PC.
architect

BUILDINGS R US
engineers

mechanical unit - see mechanical

roof protection pavers

roof hatch

DB-3-2 typ.

DB-3-3 typ.

duct down

elevator penthouse - provide ⅛" per foot min. slope

fan curb - see mech.

provide crickets such that min slope of ⅛" per foot is maintained

skylight

GENERAL NOTES
· all dimensions are to face of framing member

ISSUE:

DATE:

ROOF PLAN

A-4

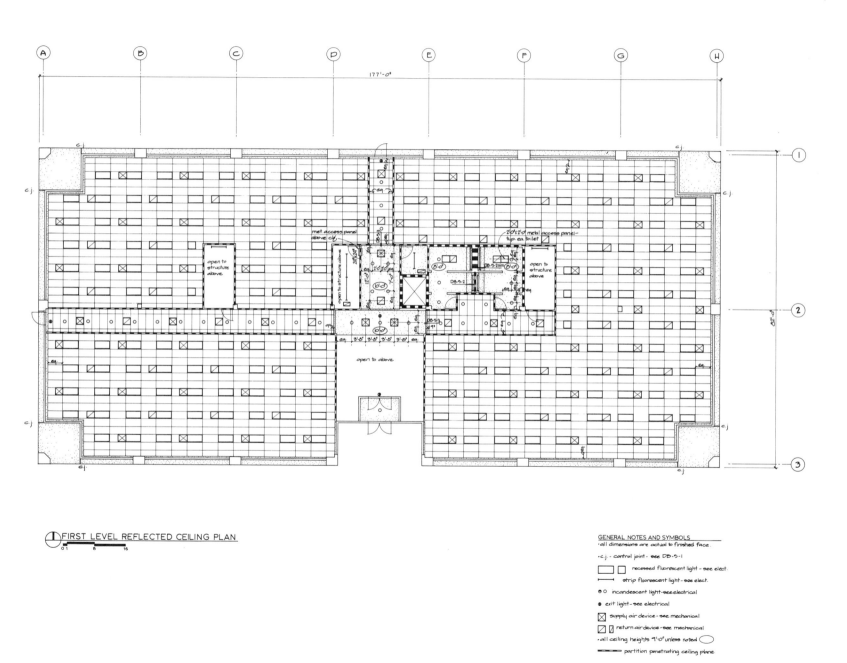

A
B
C
D
E
F
G
H

177'-0"

c.j.
c.j.
c.j.
c.j.

1
2
3

open to
structure
above

open to
structure
above

open to
structure
above

open to above

met. access panel
above c.j.

2'0"x12"d metal access panel-
typ. ea. toilet

DB-5-2sm

DB-5-2

eq. 3'-0" 3'-0" 3'-0" 3'-0" eq.

c.j.
c.j.
c.j.

① FIRST LEVEL REFLECTED CEILING PLAN

0 1   8   16

A
SPECULATIVE
OFFICE
BUILDING
in
DUGONE COUNTY
for

NICHOLAS
PROPERTIES

GENW, PC.
architect
BUILDINGS R US
engineers

ISSUE:

DATE:

FIRST LEVEL
REFLECTED
CEILING PLAN

A-5

GENERAL NOTES AND SYMBOLS
· all dimensions are actual to finished face.
· c.j. - control joint - see DB-5-1
☐ ☐ recessed fluorescent light - see elect.
├───┤ strip fluorescent light - see elect.
● ○ incandescent light - see electrical
● exit light - see electrical
☒ supply air device - see mechanical
☒ ☐ return air device - see mechanical
· all ceiling heights 9'-0" unless noted ◯
▬▬▬ partition penetrating ceiling plane

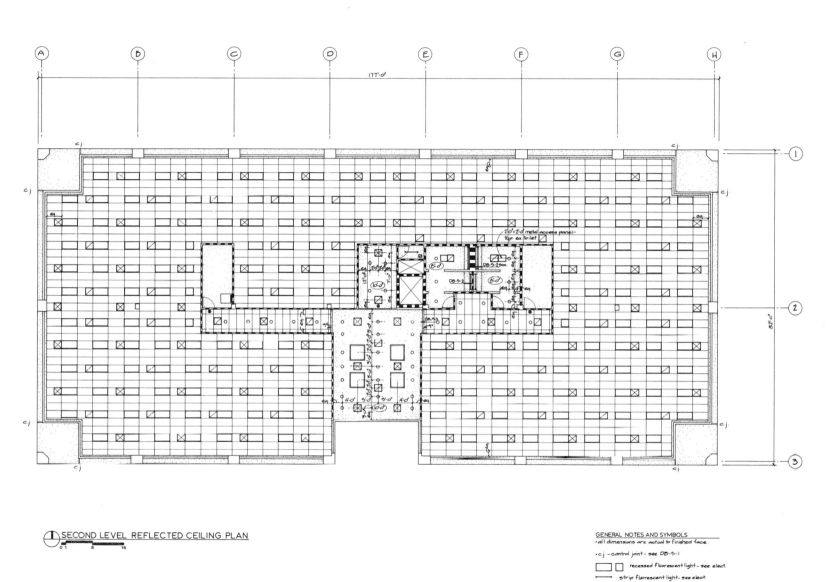

A B C D E F G H

177'-0"

c.j.

c.j.

c.j.

c.j.

c.j.

c.j.

c.j.

c.j.

82'-0"

1
2
3

2'-0" x 2'-0" metal access panel—
typ. ea. toilet

DB-5-2 sm.

DB-5-2

4'-0" 5'-0" 4'-0"

① SECOND LEVEL REFLECTED CEILING PLAN
0 1   8   16

A
SPECULATIVE
OFFICE
BUILDING
in
DUGONE COUNTY
for
NICHOLAS
PROPERTIES

GENW, PC
architect

BUILDINGS R US
engineers

ISSUE:

DATE:

SECOND LEVEL
REFLECTED
CEILING PLAN

A-6

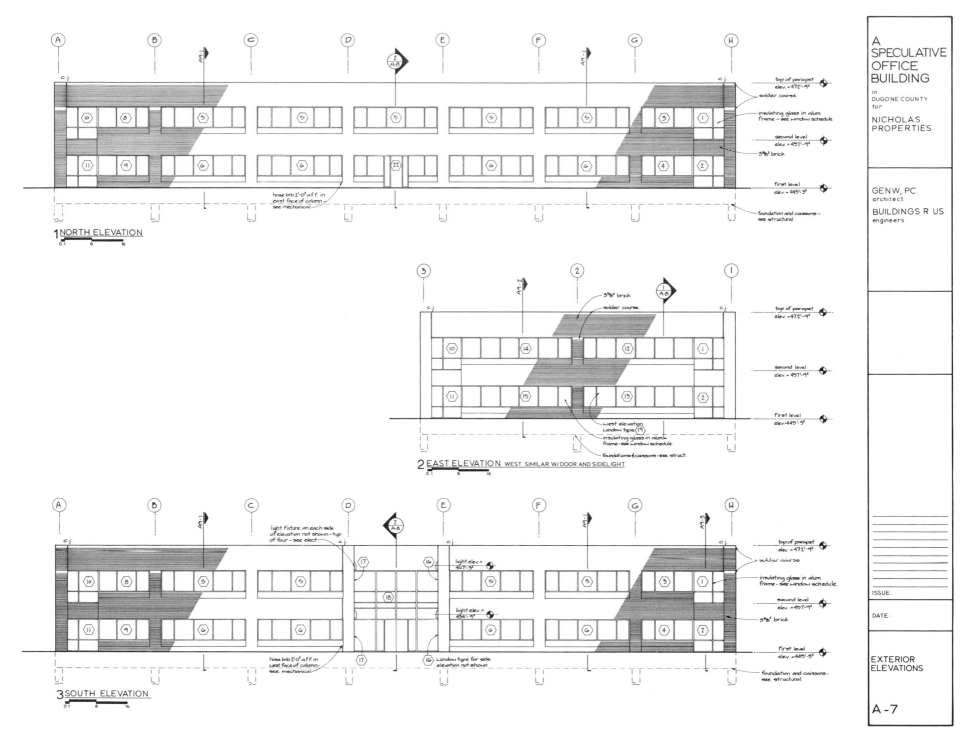

1 NORTH ELEVATION

0 1 8 16

2 EAST ELEVATION WEST SIMILAR W/ DOOR AND SIDELIGHT

0 1 8 16

3 SOUTH ELEVATION

0 1 8 16

A
SPECULATIVE
OFFICE
BUILDING
in
DUGONE COUNTY
for

NICHOLAS
PROPERTIES

GENW, PC.
architect

BUILDINGS R US
engineers

ISSUE:

DATE:

EXTERIOR
ELEVATIONS

A-7

North Elevation labels:
top of parapet elev. = 472'-9"
soldier course
insulating glass in alum. frame - see window schedule
second level elev. = 457'-9"
3⅝" brick
first level elev. = 445'-3"
hose bib 2'-0" a.f.f. in east face of column - see mechanical
foundation and caissons - see structural

East Elevation labels:
3⅝" brick
soldier course
top of parapet elev. = 472'-9"
second level elev. = 457'-9"
first level elev. = 445'-5"
west elevation window type (19)
insulating glass in alum. frame - see window schedule
foundation & caissons - see struct.

South Elevation labels:
light fixture on each side of elevation not shown - typ of four - see elect.
top of parapet elev. = 472'-9"
soldier course
insulating glass in alum. frame - see window schedule
light elev. = 467'-3"
second level elev. = 457'-9"
3⅝" brick
light elev. = 454'-9"
first level elev. = 445'-9"
hose bib 2'-0" a.f.f. in west face of column - see mechanical
window type for side elevation not shown
foundation and caissons - see structural

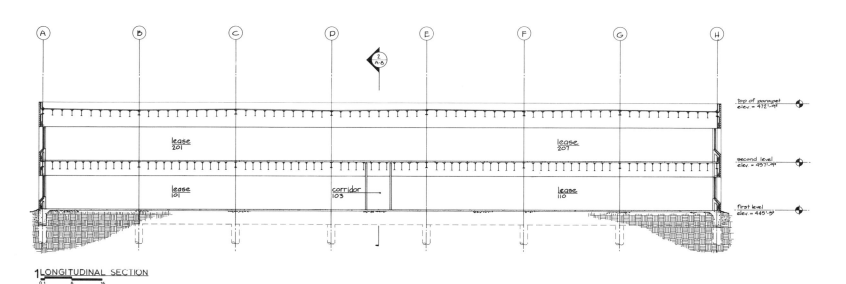

A
B
C
D
E
F
G
H

2
A-8

top of parapet
elev. = 472'-9"

lease
201

lease
207

second level
elev. = 457'-9"

lease
101

corridor
103

lease
110

first level
elev. = 445'-3"

1 LONGITUDINAL SECTION

0 1   8   16

1
2
3

1
A-8

skylights beyond

thread ductwork thru joists as
necy. at ceilings of lobby 113, elev.
lobby 203 + 105 - see mechanical

top of parapet
elev. = 472'-9"

verify type and size
of curb - see mech.
and struct.

elev. lobby
203

lease
201

lobby
113

second level
elev. = 457'-9"

vest.
114

elev. lobby
105

corridor
103

first level
elev. = 445'-3"

2 TRANSVERSE SECTION

0 1   8   16

A
SPECULATIVE
OFFICE
BUILDING
in
DUGONE COUNTY
for
NICHOLAS
PROPERTIES

GEN W, PC.
architect
BUILDINGS R US
engineers

ISSUE:

DATE:

BUILDING
SECTIONS

A-8

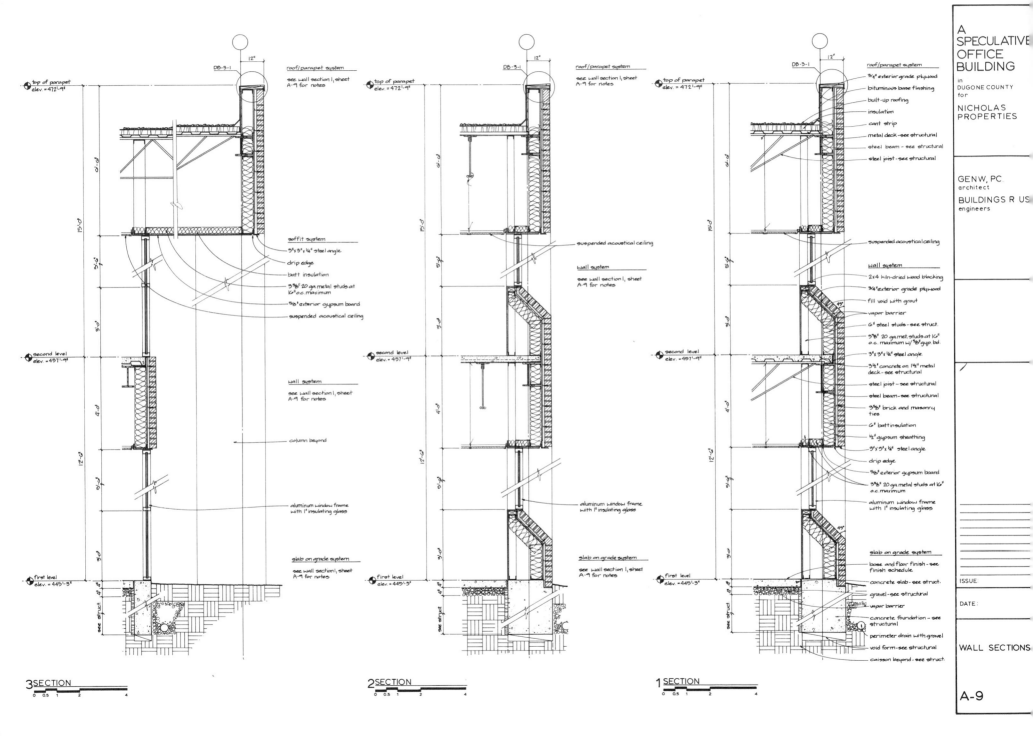

A SPECULATIVE OFFICE BUILDING
in DUGONE COUNTY
for
NICHOLAS PROPERTIES

GENW, PC
architect

BUILDINGS R US
engineers

ISSUE:

DATE:

WALL SECTIONS

A-9

Section 3 (left)

top of parapet
elev. = 472'-9"

DB-3-1
12"

roof/parapet system
see wall section 1, sheet A-9 for notes

soffit system
- 3"x 3"x ¼" steel angle
- drip edge
- batt insulation
- 3⅝" 20 ga. metal studs at 16" o.c. maximum
- ⅝" exterior gypsum board
- suspended acoustical ceiling

second level
elev. = 457'-9"

wall system
see wall section 1, sheet A-9 for notes

column beyond

aluminum window frame with 1" insulating glass

slab on grade system
see wall section 1, sheet A-9 for notes

first level
elev. = 445'-3"

3 SECTION
0 0.5 1 2 4

Section 2 (middle)

top of parapet
elev. = 472'-9"

DB-3-1
12"

roof/parapet system
see wall section 1, sheet A-9 for notes

suspended acoustical ceiling

wall system
see wall section 1, sheet A-9 for notes

second level
elev. = 457'-9"

aluminum window frame with 1" insulating glass

slab on grade system
see wall section 1, sheet A-9 for notes

first level
elev. = 445'-3"

2 SECTION
0 0.5 1 2 4

Section 1 (right)

top of parapet
elev. = 472'-9"

DB-3-1
12"

roof/parapet system
- ¾" exterior grade plywood
- bituminous base flashing
- built-up roofing
- insulation
- cant strip
- metal deck - see structural
- steel beam - see structural
- steel joist - see structural

suspended acoustical ceiling

wall system
- 2x4 kiln-dried wood blocking
- ¾" exterior grade plywood
- fill void with grout
- vapor barrier
- 6" steel studs - see struct.
- 3⅝" 20 ga. metal studs at 16" o.c. maximum w/ ⅝" gyp. bd.
- 3"x 3"x ¼" steel angle
- 3½" concrete on 1½" metal deck - see structural
- steel joist - see structural
- steel beam - see structural
- 3⅝" brick and masonry ties
- 6" batt insulation
- ½" gypsum sheathing
- 3"x 3"x ¼" steel angle
- drip edge
- ⅝" exterior gypsum board
- 3⅝" 20 ga. metal studs at 16" o.c. maximum

second level
elev. = 457'-9"

aluminum window frame with 1" insulating glass

slab on grade system
- base and floor finish - see finish schedule
- concrete slab - see struct.
- gravel - see structural
- vapor barrier
- concrete foundation - see structural
- perimeter drain with gravel
- void form - see structural
- caisson beyond - see struct.

first level
elev. = 445'-3"

1 SECTION
0 0.5 1 2 4

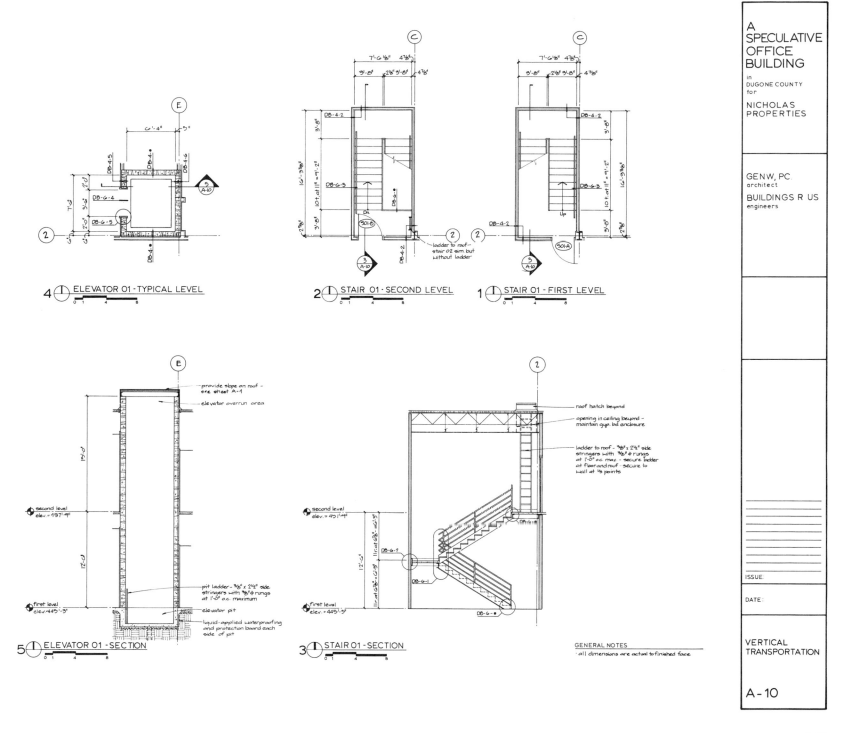

4 ELEVATOR 01 - TYPICAL LEVEL
0 1 4 8

2 STAIR 01 - SECOND LEVEL
0 1 4 8

1 STAIR 01 - FIRST LEVEL
0 1 4 8

ladder to roof -
stair 02 sim but
without ladder

5 ELEVATOR 01 - SECTION
0 1 4 8

provide slope on roof -
see sheet A-9

elevator overrun area

second level
elev. = 457'-4"

first level
elev. = 445'-3"

pit ladder - ⅜" x 2½" side
stringers with ⅜"∅ rungs
at 1'-0" o.c. maximum

elevator pit

liquid-applied waterproofing
and protection board each
side of pit

3 STAIR 01 - SECTION
0 1 4 8

roof hatch beyond

opening in ceiling beyond -
maintain gyp. bd. enclosure

ladder to roof - ⅜" x 2½" side
stringers with ⅜"∅ rungs
at 1'-0" o.c. max - secure ladder
at floor and roof - secure to
wall at ⅓ points

second level
elev. = 457'-4"

first level
elev. = 445'-3"

GENERAL NOTES
· all dimensions are actual to finished face

A
SPECULATIVE
OFFICE
BUILDING
in
DUGONE COUNTY
for

NICHOLAS
PROPERTIES

GENW, PC.
architect

BUILDINGS R US
engineers

ISSUE:

DATE:

VERTICAL
TRANSPORTATION

A-10

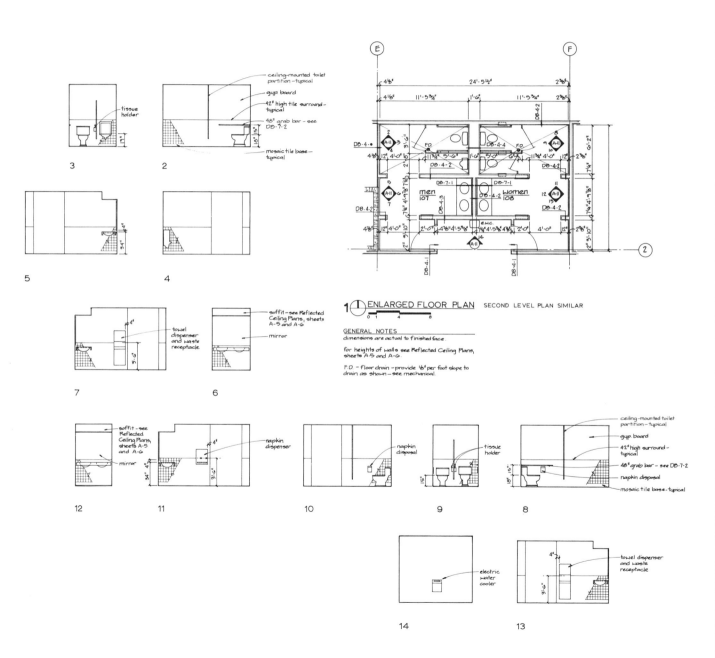

3

2

ceiling-mounted toilet partition – typical

gyp.board

42" high tile surround – typical

48" grab bar – see DB-7-2

mosaic tile base – typical

tissue holder

5

4

7

6

soffit – see Reflected Ceiling Plans, sheets A-5 and A-6

towel dispenser and waste receptacle

mirror

12

11

10

9

8

soffit – see Reflected Ceiling Plans, sheets A-5 and A-6

mirror

napkin dispenser

napkin disposal

tissue holder

ceiling-mounted toilet partition – typical

gyp.board

42" high surround – typical

48" grab bar – see DB-7-2

napkin disposal

mosaic tile base – typical

14

13

electric water cooler

towel dispenser and waste receptacle

E   F

24'-5¾"

men 107   women 108

DB-7-1   DB-7-1

DB-4-2

encl.

2

1 ENLARGED FLOOR PLAN   SECOND LEVEL PLAN SIMILAR

0 1   4   8

GENERAL NOTES
dimensions are actual to finished face.

for heights of walls see Reflected Ceiling Plans, sheets A-5 and A-6.

F.D. – floor drain – provide ⅛" per foot slope to drain as shown – see mechanical.

A
SPECULATIVE
OFFICE
BUILDING
in
DUGONE COUNTY
for
NICHOLAS
PROPERTIES

GENW, PC
architect
BUILDINGS R US
engineers

ISSUE:

DATE:

ENLARGED
PLANS AND
INTERIOR
ELEVATIONS

A-11

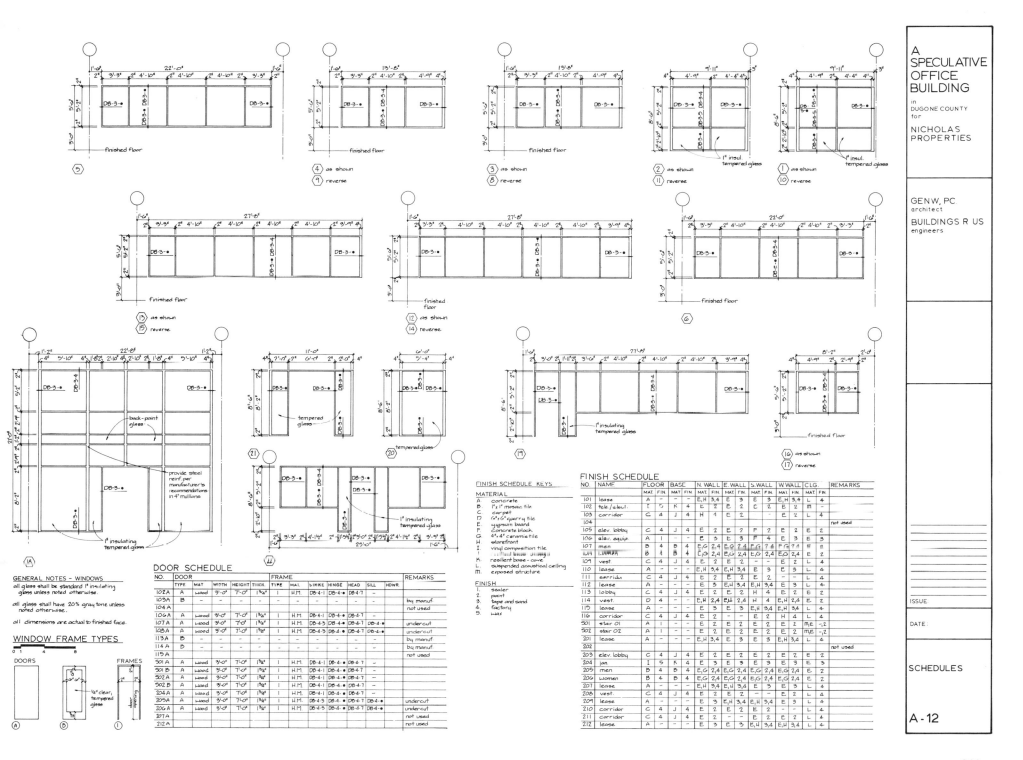

Index

Senior Editor: Cornelia Guest
Designer: Bob Fillie
Production Manager: Hector Campbell
Set in 10-point ITC Franklin Gothic Book